COMPUTER
PROJECT
MANAGEMENT

Computing Sciences Series
Editor: S. J. Orebi Gann

COMPUTER PROJECT MANAGEMENT

COLIN BENTLEY

Colin Bentley Associates Limited
Waterlooville, Hampshire, UK

A Wiley Heyden Publication

JOHN WILEY & SONS

Chichester · New York · Brisbane · Toronto · Singapore

British Library Cataloguing in Publication Data
Bentley, Colin
   Computer project management.—(Computing science
   series)
   1. Electronic data processing—Management
   2. Industrial project management
   I. Title   II. Series
   658.4'04   QA76.9.M3

   ISBN 0 471 26208 0

First published 1982 by Heyden & Son Ltd.,
Reprinted 1984, Copyright © Wiley Heyden Ltd.

Printed in Northern Ireland at the Universities Press (Belfast) Ltd.

CONTENTS

FOREWORD

Computing science has now progressed so far that it is no longer the exclusive preserve of the research specialist but extends into everyday life, from the microchip which controls the modern washing machine to a company's accounts or word-processing operations. The width, scope and impact of the subject will continue to expand during the 1980s and the purpose of this series is to chart the changes with a set of monographs and other extended works which will enable the reader to understand the effects and the potential of any key features and exciting developments in the field.

The level has been chosen to appeal to both the seasoned data processing professional who wishes to keep abreast of his subject, and to the informed layman such as the line manager, who is likely to be the end user of commercial computer systems and who wishes to appreciate the possible benefits and disadvantages in his work and even, nowadays, in his leisure activities.

A project is the job of producing some end result, which may be a computer system, or something totally different such as an oil refinery. It could equally be concerned with the production of something less tangible such as staging a concert.

Unfortunately, projects frequently suffer two major disasters; they run late and they cost more than was originally expected. In many instances, with the benefit of hindsight, it can be seen that the project would never have been started if the final cost and timescale had been correctly estimated at the outset. In other cases, a project may be found to go out of control, which basically means that heavy, unexpected expenditure is required merely to maintain an appearance of progress.

Such problems are not inevitable. A well structured formal approach to the management of projects, irrespective of their size, will allow monitoring of progress and costs against the planned position and will give advance notice of serious difficulties, allowing suitable action to be taken to minimize the effect. The result is a project which is more likely to run to schedule and to meet its budget.

This book is written by a practising project manager and describes the methodology of successful planning and project control, detailing the involvement needed by both the project team and the end user of the system at the different stages of a project. The techniques are particularly relevant to the production of the complex computer systems which will be required in the next decade as User departments begin to appreciate the full potential of the technological advances which are now being made.

November 1981   S. J. Orebi Gann

PREFACE

My early years in computing were spent without the benefit of training in project management. I was taught programming languages, flowcharting, how to operate a computer, and how to use utility programs provided by the manufacturer. Quite a lot of this time was spent being taught things which I would use rarely, if ever. The often-voiced criticism was 'if ever I need that facility, I will be able to recognize it, and I can look it up'. That is one of the big differences between programming and project management. In project management, it is far more difficult to recognize needs in advance, far more difficult to look up the precise answer in a book, and reacting to a problem now is likely to be much more expensive than having foreseen it in a plan. In my early days of project management, I made a lot of expensive mistakes through not having good standards to which to work. I trust that this book provides guidelines which will enable readers to avoid some of the pitfalls and lessen the impact of any mistakes. Readers should find the checklists and documentation standards particularly useful on a day-to-day basis, but please remember that without planning and then controlling against your plan, a lot of time and money can disappear down the drain.

Project management methods are having to keep up with developments in computing. I am now involved in looking ahead at what changes will be needed to manage a project, in a 'prototyping' or 'systems evolution' mode, making use of many of the new program development aids now on the market. More automated aids to planning and control are also appearing on the market: an obvious area for improvement.

Finally, before releasing you to the tender mercies of the book, may I acknowledge my debt to two companies who taught me a lot about project management; IBM and Simpact Systems Ltd.

London   Colin Bentley
November 1981

ix

1 INTRODUCTION

This book on project management is written by a practising project manager, who has tried to define a simple structure suitable for any environment and any size of project, including maintenance tasks.

WHY?

There are still many data processing groups which operate without recognized and formally defined standards covering the definition of their development work. They can usually be recognized by their inability to meet schedules or budget targets, the lack of project status awareness by their management, and the regular re-invention of the wheel. They need standards, and this book sets out to provide a good, well-proven basis for those standards.

There is another group of program or system developers which also needs a low-cost solution to project management standards. Increasingly, through the advent of microcomputers, more and more systems are being developed outside formal, well-established data processing groups. Even users themselves are taking on the development of increasingly complex programs. This book aims to explain the necessity of planning in the management of such projects to a successful conclusion and providing a solution.

The idea of formal structures and disciplines often creates a mental image of bureaucratic overkill, extra expense and time wasted in meetings or preparing reports. This author has never seen a set of good project management standards lose time or money by their implementation. They do cost time and money, and this must be added to the cost of the project. However, overall they save money, as development without them will almost inevitably mean a project which overruns both schedule and budget, and is unsatisfactory to the user.

The three principal objectives of this book are:

to explain the need for project management standards,

to provide a structure of the required standards,
to provide detailed standards within this structure.

LIMITATIONS

Project management standards can be employed by very large or very small groups. This book attempts to offer a general solution which will work for all sizes of group and all sizes of project. In attempting to cover such a wide span, there may be times when the person interested only in small projects will feel that the standard is being described in too much detail. This book tries to identify such occasions and explain how those dealing with a small project should approach that particular standard. If no abbreviation or avoidance is suggested, however, the reader should be wary of ignoring any components of the standards. It may be necessary to complete certain operations under the standards in order to avoid later problems or common mistakes, even though the work seems too trivial to warrant the extra effort.

SOLUTION

In this book, the approach to project management standards is divided into a number of headings, each representing one of the key areas where standards are needed. Figure 1.1 illustrates this structure.

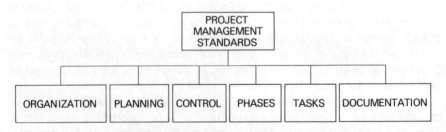

Fig. 1.1 Overview of project management standards areas.

Organization

Although this title may seem rather grand when considering the development of a small system, it is always important to define, and make sure that everyone understands, who has what responsibilities to the project, who is going to do what, and who has what authority. Such questions cover who is to define the requirements. Since many projects fail because the requirements were never clearly and fully written down at the outset, this is vital to any size of project. They also cover questions which may arise in any project, such as who has the authority to change or add to the requirements, who is going to pay for development and changes to the requirements, who reports to whom, who is responsible for preparing the files for the system, and so on. In the chapter on organization, the book defines a complete structure of responsibilities and describes how these can be allocated according to different sizes of project.

Planning

All projects need planning. This book does not attempt to impose any particular methodology, such as PERT or bar charting. It does, however, define the types of plan needed, when plans are needed, and how much of the project a particular plan should cover. The chapter on planning is closely associated with the chapters on phases and tasks. The former helps the user decide into how many parts the project should be split for planning purposes, and the latter details the activities which may need to be planned in each chosen phase.

Control

A plan is of very little use unless we are going to check our progress against it at regular intervals. This is described in the chapter on control. The checking includes how and when we should compare the plan with actual progress, how to highlight any disparity, to whom reports should be made, suggested formats for such reports, and what action to take upon recognizing a disparity. The chapter also includes descriptions of the types of meeting which should be held as part of overall control, and provides agendas and checklists for them. One extra aspect of control included in the chapter is the question of controlling requests to change. Almost every project will receive requests for changes in requirements during development. If these are not very strictly controlled, they can destroy the schedule and budget of any project. It is not always possible to ignore such requests until the current project is complete, and this chapter puts forward a method of dealing with them while still keeping schedule and budget under control.

Phases

Virtually every project should be divided into a number of parts. Each part is concerned with a major activity, such as the definition of requirements. In this book, these parts are called 'phases'. For even the smallest of projects, it is advisable to separate the development of a solution from its installation. There are a number of reasons for breaking a project up. The project may be so big that it is impossible to plan in detail in one piece. The responsibility for the next major task may change hands. For example, after a solution has been developed and is about to be installed, the installer takes responsibility for preparing the data to be used, the physical area to be used, and the people to be used. The major reason for dividing a project into parts is to control the allocation of funds and resources to the project. The payer can then release only a portion of the total cost at a time, the amount defined in the next phase plan, and only release those funds on satisfactory completion of the previous phase. The book describes a very flexible approach to the number of phases needed for a specific project. This chapter closely relates to the chapter on tasks.

Tasks

This chapter contains checklists of activities required in any project. The lists relate to the phases defined in the previous chapter, and are therefore presented at a number of levels of detail. The planner selects the appropriate level of detail for the project in hand.

Documentation

No project can succeed without documentation, and many projects fail through poor documentation at one or more points in the project. This chapter defines an overall structure for a project's documentation from requirements to user manual and the documentation of tests. Each volume and chapter is defined in detail, and formats are given where applicable. The philosophy behind the documentation is one of gradual development, and the avoidance of duplication and unnecessary documentation. The approach lends itself to the use of word processors in the preparation of the documentation.

The content of each chapter is presented in the same basic sequence with the aim of giving a consistent and complete picture of each aspect of successful project management.

2 ORGANIZATION

This chapter discusses the question of who should be involved in a project, and proposes a structure to allow the full representation and participation of all parties. It examines the need of both user and DP management to monitor a project and keep overall control, without the need for day-to-day involvement. The need for and provision of communication channels is also defined and linked with the organization standards proposed: no organization standard can work without clearly defined internal and external communication channels.

WHY?

Why do we need to establish a formal organization structure?

1   In any industry or profession, organizing and coordinating projects have always been difficult management tasks. Organization standards will help us in task delegation and setting up the necessary project internal communications.

2   Data processing does not have a history of good communication with its users. Too often, after the original request for a solution, the user has felt excluded from the project until the final solution is presented. We need a standard which defines when and how the user can maintain participation in the project in order to ensure that the right solution is produced.

3   Top management cannot personally control every project in a busy, multi-project environment. An organization standard will define how authority can be delegated while overall control is maintained.

4   There is a considerable difference between the tasks of line management and project management. A formal organization structure will help define these differences and the points at which the two interface.

5   It is the user's money which is being spent on the project and therefore

5

user management must be represented when decisions on expenditure are being made.

6   If small projects are being used to give non-management a training ground in leadership, management must have a formal way of keeping an eye on them.

7   A well-organized project can avoid arguments on who does what, forgotten tasks, and difficulty in knowing the project status.

8   There is a great need for a method of gradually developing leadership skills. Today, most Project Leaders arrive at their position because they have been good technicians. Good technicians may not necessarily be good leaders, and there will have been no method of evaluating their leadership skills in a practical environment. Too often, the first indication of any lack of skill is when we have a disastrous project on our hands. Organization standards can define the career path, skills and experience to be acquired to develop leadership skills in the project staff gradually.

9   On larger projects, one person may be unable to handle the roles of technical leadership, administration, and business planning and control. A standard is needed which will identify how these different roles can be divided and allocated to different people if required.

OBJECTIVES

1   To define standard job descriptions to cover the various standard roles in a project.

2   To define overall management control of a project.

3   To define the bodies which need to be represented in overall control of a project.

4   To define the role of user management in a project.

5   To give guidance to user and DP management when they are considering who should be on the managing body of a project.

6   To permit management by objectives and management by exception.

7   To cover the allocation of responsibilities for phase planning, phase reporting, team leadership, technical expertise, setting Team Member objectives, appraisal of Team Members against objectives, and delegation of responsibility and/or authority.

8   To provide clear separation of the technical and administrative skill needed in project leadership.

9   To define a standard which would allow a non-DP person to be a Project Leader for certain phases of a project.

10 To assemble the right skills in the project group at the right time.

11 To provide a method of communicating between the project group and external bodies, such as the user and DP operations.

12 To provide a method of communicating within the group involved in a project. Communication entails allocating tasks and responsibilities, reporting status, agreeing target dates, avoiding duplication of effort, and disseminating information.

13 To show us what training our people need in order to play a specific role in a project.

14 To develop a Project Team philosophy which will help us plan the work experience needed in the career progression of our staff.

15 To devise a structure which will provide gradual entry into and training in project leadership.

LIMITATIONS

1 The organization structure must fit in with other project standards.

2 The standard must recognize that user and DP line management have other work to do.

3 The standard must keep extra paperwork to a minimum.

4 It should be possible to tailor the approach to individual company environments.

5 The standard must be applicable to both large and small projects.

SOLUTION

To be successful, the organization structure of a project must encompass two key areas:

Decision making
Communications

These are important for any type of project. There is a third area which is dependent on the type of project:

Tasks

The following solution offers a structure which defines the necessary roles to be taken in a project. The responsibility for the various decisions is clearly allocated to the roles, and communication paths between the roles are defined. These two points are discussed further in Chapter 4, which defines the information which should be passed along these communication paths, leading to the relevant decisions.

Throughout the chapter, it will be stressed that the solution talks about roles. According to the size of the project, these roles are shared out to different numbers of people, giving a flexible format which can be applied to large or small projects. It should be stressed here that each role must be taken by someone, even in a very small project.

Organization structure

Figure 2.1 shows a hierarchy which can be used as the basis of a solution to meet all the objectives of this chapter. For maximum flexibility, it makes use of Project Teams. There are different levels of authority and responsibility in a project. There are also different tasks to be performed in a given sequence during a project. As we progress through a project, the skills required to perform these tasks change. We can use these changes to define a notional set of teams to be employed in sequence. Members of staff can now be moved from team to team, within the same project or to another, from level to level as the need arises and still find themselves within a defined work specification. This allows flexibility which is under control.

The Planning Committee's functions are forward planning and project initiation. It delegates management responsibility for the project to a Project Board.

The Project Board is composed of representatives of contractor and user management. It is not normally involved in running the project on a day-to-day basis. Its mission is to monitor project progress and make key decisions on resource use.

Fig. 2.1 Project Team hierarchy.

Project Management, on a day-to-day basis, is in the hands of the Project Leader.

The Phase Team assists the Project Leader.

Planning Committee

At the top of our team hierarchy, we need a group whose function is to look ahead at the company's three- or five-year plan, and to devise a strategy to complement it. In which direction is the company going? What products or systems will it need to support its progress? What equipment policy should be followed? What are the user priorities? This group is also charged with the responsibility of ensuring that the maximum amount of compatibility exists between systems developed. Such a group must include:

high-level user management,
representatives of the general company management.

Major tasks for the Planning Committee are:

deciding equipment policy;
monitoring resources and their capacity to meet user demands;
coordination of all user requests for project effort;
initiation of any feasibility studies and allocation of resources to these studies;
monitoring all project status;
appointment, together with the user, of a management body to control a project;
agreement with the appropriate line management on the deployment of a member of staff as Project Leader for a feasibility study.

Project Board

Figure 2.2 shows the proposed construction of the Project Board. It is easy to understand how this will work for larger projects. However, does every small piece of maintenance work need a three-man Project Board? Obviously, if we are to meet the objectives stated at the beginning of the chapter, there must be an easy solution. With small projects, there are, in fact, at least two possible ways of implementing this.

Firstly, although there are three roles to be played on the Project Board, it is possible to allocate more than one role to the same person. For a small project, the user might also take the chairman's role.

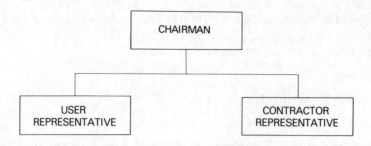

Fig. 2.2   Structure of the Project Board.

A second possibility is as follows. Many small projects are generated by an existing production system. In view of the investment in that system, and the importance of its continued performance, it would be wise to appoint a permanent or semi-permanent group which would act as a Project Board for all the maintenance and enhancement projects for that product. Thus, at their meetings the Project Board might be reviewing several projects at the same time.

Project Management

Figure 2.3 expands the concept of a team responsible for the day-to-day management of the project. The roles to be filled are:

Project Leader
Team Leader
Back-up
Project Administrator

It must be stressed here that these are the necessary roles to be played. It is not always required to have a different person to play each role. Depending on the size of the project (even a particular phase) we can allocate more than one role to the same person. Another way of allocation is, for example, that one person might act as Project Administrator to a number of small projects.

The Project Leader has managerial status, and is responsible for task allocation, objective-setting, budget preparation, and appraisal of Team Members at the end of a phase. The Team Leader is the technical leader, advising the Project Leader on technical matters, and helping the Project Leader to create reasonable technical plans. The Team Leader is also responsible for quality of work from the Phase Team. The Back-up is the Team Leader's support on larger projects in quality control. A main task for the Back-up is the provision of tools and techniques to the Phase

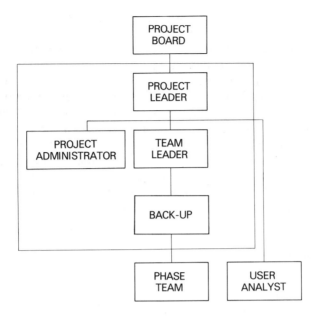

Fig. 2.3   Structure of the Project Management Team.

Team to carry out their work. On smaller projects, this role may also be carried out by the Team Leader, but it is useful to use this role as an early training ground for people who will later be given the chance to be Team Leaders.

The Project Administrator has a mainly clerical role. It can be an inexpensive way of taking the simpler, repetitive tasks off the shoulders of the Project Team Leaders. It is also a way of providing expertise in certain fields in which Project Leaders may be totally unskilled, such as financial plan preparation.

Detailed function descriptions for all the Project Management Team are given at the end of this chapter.

There are two other areas of our organization structure to be considered:

User Analyst
Phase Team

User Analyst

As well as user representation at Project Board level, we need the user's involvement on a regular basis at a working level. The involvement has two sides; the provision and clarification of user needs, and the monitoring of the solution as it emerges. This role can vary in size from a part-time task for one person, up to one needing a team of User Analysts. The formal definition of the role makes the communication and liaison between contractor and user clear. It also defines the tasks to be carried out by the User Analyst function in each phase. There would therefore be a different function description for each phase. The User Analyst is the normal link with user management. It is the role of the User Analyst to interpret the user requirements as defined by user management at the beginning of the project, to expand these requirements to a detailed level, and to monitor the development of a solution against these requirements. The User Analyst will not normally have the authority to request extra facilities or agree to the dropping of previously requested facilities.

Phase Team

The tasks and end products of each phase of a project differ, and therefore the skills needed vary from phase to phase. We therefore need a different team for each phase. This is not the same question as how big a team we need. That will depend mainly on the project size. Our standard should define the skills needed, one role for each different skill. At the end of this chapter, a possible Feasibility Phase Team is described as an example. It must be emphasized that these are the necessary roles to be played. It is not always required to have a separate person to play each role.

We can standardize on the information needed in order to define our team and individual missions. Figure 2.4 is an example of a form for this purpose. The two parts of the form are used together to define each type of role to be performed. They are completed in the following way.

Team	The name of the team fulfilling this role.
Team Member	The title of the role. This is left blank if the form relates to the whole team.
Team Structure	A hierarchical diagram of all the roles in the team, showing levels of authority.
Mission	A brief description of the overall purpose of the team.
Communications	Notes on external interfaces, from whom and to whom direction is given, frequency of formal communication, and method of communication.
Required Experience	A description of the work experience and/or qualifications required before being suitable to perform this role.

Required Training	A description of the formal training required before being suitable to perform this role.
Tasks	A list of the tasks to be performed by this role. The task description should make it clear if any other party is involved in the task, the relationship between the role and the others involved, and any standard or technique to be used in performing the task.

In several places on the forms, we can cross-refer to other project standards. We can do this in 'Communication', 'Required Training' and 'Tasks', where we can refer to documentation standards, forms to be used, techniques etc.

In the sample job/role descriptions following Fig. 2.4, one pair of these forms is used to define the mission of the team, followed by a completed pair of forms for each role to be performed within that team.

To give a clearer idea of the use of these pages and the team concept, the following pages contain examples of Team and Team Member missions (or job function specifications, if you prefer those titles). The examples taken are the Project Board (Fig. 2.5), the Project Management Team (Fig. 2.9) and the team for the first phase, Feasibility (Fig. 2.14).

TEAM
TEAM MEMBER
TEAM STRUCTURE
MISSION
COMMUNICATIONS
REQUIRED EXPERIENCE
REQUIRED TRAINING

Fig. 2.4   Team/Team Member mission (page 1).

TEAM

TEAM MEMBER

TASKS

Fig. 2.4   (cont.) (page 2).

TEAM	Project Board

TEAM MEMBER

TEAM STRUCTURE

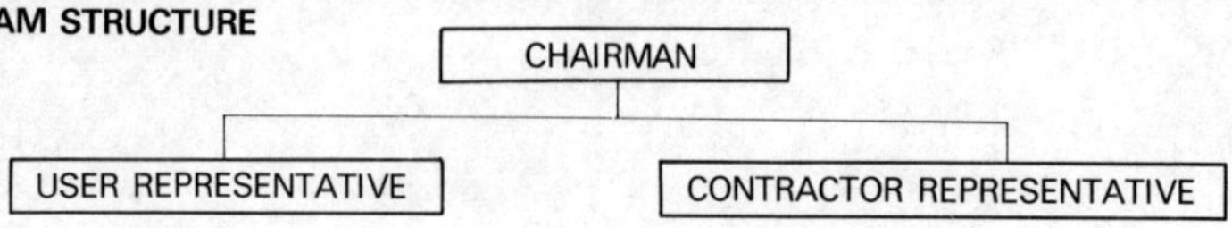

```
                    ┌─────────────┐
                    │  CHAIRMAN   │
                    └─────────────┘
          ┌────────────────┴────────────────┐
┌──────────────────────┐          ┌──────────────────────────────┐
│ USER REPRESENTATIVE   │          │ CONTRACTOR REPRESENTATIVE    │
└──────────────────────┘          └──────────────────────────────┘
```

MISSION

Overall direction and control of the project.
The Project Board represents the user and contractor management,
and reports to both managements on behalf of the project.

COMMUNICATIONS

REQUIRED EXPERIENCE

1   Company managerial role.
2   Knowledge of the area which they represent.

REQUIRED TRAINING

1   Project management standards overview.
2   Organization standards.

Fig. 2.5   Project Board mission.

TEAM   Project Board

TEAM MEMBER

TASKS

1 To appoint the Project Leader.

2 To approve all project plans and agree appropriate tolerances.

3 To approve all deviations (outside the prescribed tolerances) from the above plan.

4 To review and approve the various 'end-products', including any resulting off-specifications.

5 To authorize the project to continue at each phase.

6 To authorize the project termination, should a satisfactory business case cease to exist for the project.

7 To arbitrate over points of difference.

8 To provide functional direction to the project via the Project Leader.

9 To provide a means to call for independent examination of the project 'end-products'.

Fig. 2.5   (cont.)

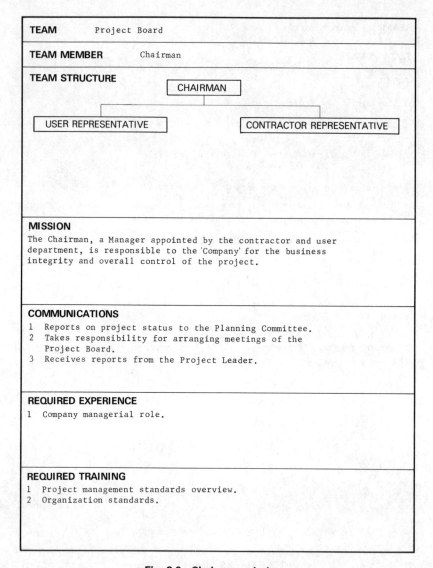

TEAM   Project Board

TEAM MEMBER   Chairman

TEAM STRUCTURE

MISSION

The Chairman, a Manager appointed by the contractor and user department, is responsible to the 'Company' for the business integrity and overall control of the project.

COMMUNICATIONS

1   Reports on project status to the Planning Committee.
2   Takes responsibility for arranging meetings of the Project Board.
3   Receives reports from the Project Leader.

REQUIRED EXPERIENCE

1   Company managerial role.

REQUIRED TRAINING

1   Project management standards overview.
2   Organization standards.

Fig. 2.6   Chairman mission.

TEAM	Project Board
TEAM MEMBER	Chairman

TASKS

1 To chair Project Board meetings.

2 To approve project plans and budgets.

3 To approve the end-products of each phase.

4 To approve action to continue, complete or terminate the project, as appropriate.

5 To take special interest in the feasibility study.

6 To prepare a report at the end of each phase from the board to the Planning Committee.

Fig. 2.6 (cont.)

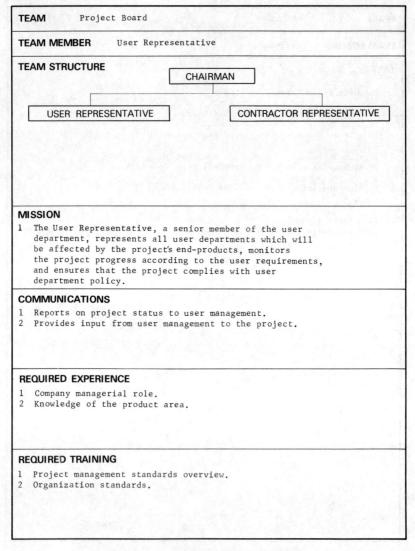

TEAM   Project Board

TEAM MEMBER   User Representative

TEAM STRUCTURE

```
                          ┌─────────────┐
                          │  CHAIRMAN   │
                          └─────────────┘
              ┌──────────────────┴──────────────────┐
  ┌───────────────────────────┐      ┌─────────────────────────────────┐
  │   USER  REPRESENTATIVE     │      │  CONTRACTOR REPRESENTATIVE      │
  └───────────────────────────┘      └─────────────────────────────────┘
```

MISSION

1 The User Representative, a senior member of the user
   department, represents all user departments which will
   be affected by the project's end-products, monitors
   the project progress according to the user requirements,
   and ensures that the project complies with user
   department policy.

COMMUNICATIONS

1 Reports on project status to user management.
2 Provides input from user management to the project.

REQUIRED EXPERIENCE

1 Company managerial role.
2 Knowledge of the product area.

REQUIRED TRAINING

1 Project management standards overview.
2 Organization standards.

Fig. 2.7 User Representative mission.

TEAM	Project Board

TEAM MEMBER	User Representative

TASKS

1 To attend project meetings on behalf of the user.

2 To resolve user requirements and priority conflicts.

3 To assign user resources required by the project.

4 To ensure that the user requirements are fully met.

5 To take a special interest in the user specification
and the installation phases.

Fig. 2.7 (cont.)

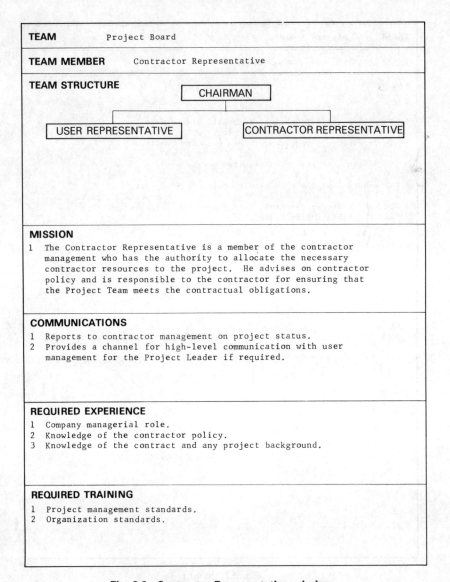

TEAM   Project Board

TEAM MEMBER   Contractor Representative

TEAM STRUCTURE

MISSION

1 The Contractor Representative is a member of the contractor
   management who has the authority to allocate the necessary
   contractor resources to the project. He advises on contractor
   policy and is responsible to the contractor for ensuring that
   the Project Team meets the contractual obligations.

COMMUNICATIONS

1 Reports to contractor management on project status.
2 Provides a channel for high-level communication with user
   management for the Project Leader if required.

REQUIRED EXPERIENCE

1 Company managerial role.
2 Knowledge of the contractor policy.
3 Knowledge of the contract and any project background.

REQUIRED TRAINING

1 Project management standards.
2 Organization standards.

Fig. 2.8   Contractor Representative mission.

TEAM	Project Board

TEAM MEMBER	Contractor Representative

TASKS

1 To attend project meetings on behalf of the contractor.

2 To resolve contractor requirements and priority conflicts.

3 To assign contractor resources required by the project.

4 To ensure that the contractual requirements are fully met.

5 To have a special interest in the design and development phases.

Fig. 2.8 (cont.)

TEAM	Project Management Team

TEAM MEMBER

TEAM STRUCTURE

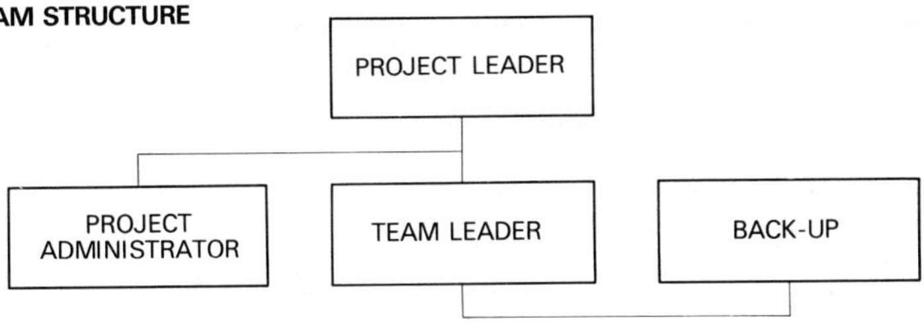

```
                    ┌──────────────────────┐
                    │    PROJECT LEADER     │
                    └──────────┬───────────┘
          ┌────────────────────┼────────────────────┐
┌───────────────────┐ ┌──────────────────┐ ┌──────────────────┐
│     PROJECT       │ │   TEAM LEADER     │ │     BACK-UP       │
│  ADMINISTRATOR    │ │                   │ │                   │
└───────────────────┘ └──────────────────┘ └──────────────────┘
```

MISSION

1 To manage the project on a day-to-day basis to
   ensure the business and the total project.

COMMUNICATIONS

1 Reports to the Project Board.
2 Provides individual plans and objectives to Team
   Members.
3 Collects status and resources usage data from Team
   Members.
4 Interfaces with the User Analyst role to maintain
   day-to-day communication with the user.
5 Interfaces with external departments at a working
   level.

REQUIRED EXPERIENCE

REQUIRED TRAINING

1 Project management standards.

Fig. 2.9 Project Management Team mission.

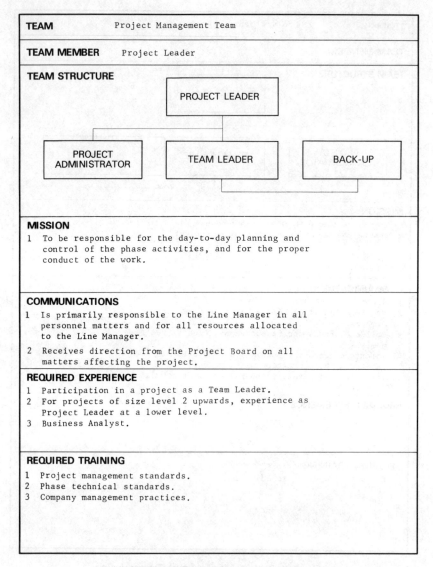

TEAM   Project Management Team

TEAM MEMBER   Project Leader

TEAM STRUCTURE

```
                          ┌─────────────────────┐
                          │   PROJECT LEADER    │
                          └─────────────────────┘
        ┌──────────────────────┬───────────────────────┐
┌───────────────┐    ┌──────────────────┐    ┌──────────────┐
│   PROJECT     │    │                  │    │              │
│ ADMINISTRATOR │    │   TEAM LEADER    │    │   BACK-UP    │
└───────────────┘    └──────────────────┘    └──────────────┘
```

MISSION

1 To be responsible for the day-to-day planning and
   control of the phase activities, and for the proper
   conduct of the work.

COMMUNICATIONS

1 Is primarily responsible to the Line Manager in all
   personnel matters and for all resources allocated
   to the Line Manager.

2 Receives direction from the Project Board on all
   matters affecting the project.

REQUIRED EXPERIENCE

1 Participation in a project as a Team Leader.
2 For projects of size level 2 upwards, experience as
   Project Leader at a lower level.
3 Business Analyst.

REQUIRED TRAINING

1 Project management standards.
2 Phase technical standards.
3 Company management practices.

Fig. 2.10 Project Leader mission.

TEAM   Project Management Team

TEAM MEMBER   Project Leader

TASKS

1 To manage the stage phase.

2 To manage allocated manpower and machine resources
   effectively.

3 To control and direct the work of the Phase Team.

4 To prepare phase activity plans, and to monitor and
   report progress against such plans to **Line** Management and the Project Board as required.

5 To provide a main liaison point with the user, and
   with specialist units in respect of technical,
   functional and operational matters related to the project.

6 To provide estimates and costs for the stage phase.

7 To ensure that the overall design and installation
   criteria and objectives as approved by the Project
   Board are fully **realized**.

8 To ensure that the project phase is conducted according
   to project management standards, and that all completed
   work conforms to the appropriate technical and
   documentation standards and is of good quality.

9 To obtain approval for all project and phase plans
   from the Project Board.

10 To report status to the Project Board on a frequency
   agreed at the last phase review.

11 To advise the Project Board immediately of any
   deviation beyond the tolerance level agreed for the
   phase plan.

Fig. 2.10   (cont.)

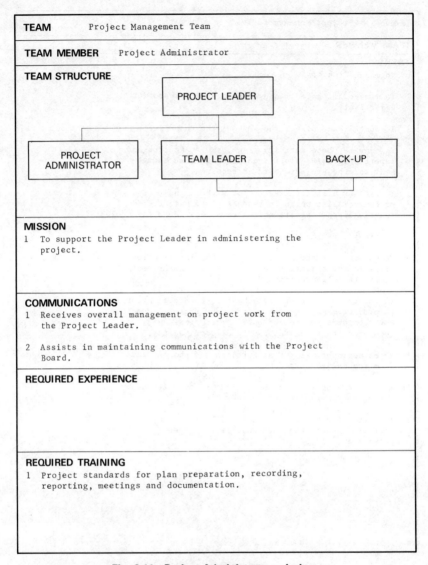

TEAM   Project Management Team

TEAM MEMBER   Project Administrator

TEAM STRUCTURE

PROJECT LEADER

PROJECT ADMINISTRATOR   TEAM LEADER   BACK-UP

MISSION
1 To support the Project Leader in administering the project.

COMMUNICATIONS
1 Receives overall management on project work from the Project Leader.

2 Assists in maintaining communications with the Project Board.

REQUIRED EXPERIENCE

REQUIRED TRAINING
1 Project standards for plan preparation, recording, reporting, meetings and documentation.

Fig. 2.11 Project Administrator mission.

TEAM	Project Management Team
TEAM MEMBER	Project Administrator

TASKS

1 To have knowledge of standard costs and overheads to be used for planning purposes.

2 To assist the Project Leader in the preparation of financial plans.

3 To gather and record actual project costs against the plan.

4 To create and maintain the project filing system

5 To act as recording secretary for project and Project Board meetings.

6 To liaise with external groups for the provision of services and supplies to the project.

7 To administer the production of project documentation, and be responsible for the safety of the master copy.

Fig. 2.11 (cont.)

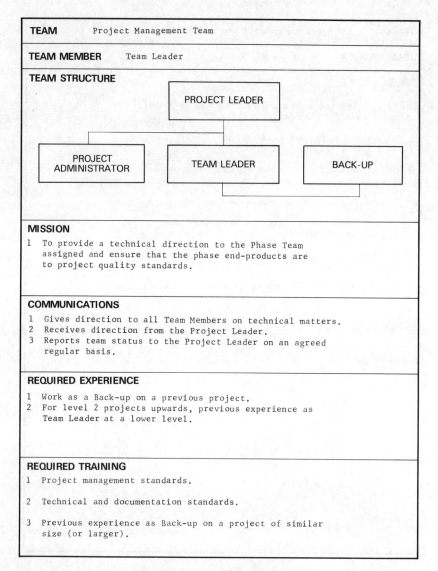

TEAM   Project Management Team

TEAM MEMBER   Team Leader

TEAM STRUCTURE

```
                    ┌─────────────────┐
                    │ PROJECT LEADER  │
                    └─────────────────┘
         ┌──────────────────┼──────────────────┐
┌─────────────────┐ ┌─────────────────┐ ┌─────────────────┐
│    PROJECT      │ │   TEAM LEADER   │ │    BACK-UP      │
│  ADMINISTRATOR  │ │                 │ │                 │
└─────────────────┘ └─────────────────┘ └─────────────────┘
```

MISSION

1 To provide a technical direction to the Phase Team
   assigned and ensure that the phase end-products are
   to project quality standards.

COMMUNICATIONS

1 Gives direction to all Team Members on technical matters.
2 Receives direction from the Project Leader.
3 Reports team status to the Project Leader on an agreed
   regular basis.

REQUIRED EXPERIENCE

1 Work as a Back-up on a previous project.
2 For level 2 projects upwards, previous experience as
   Team Leader at a lower level.

REQUIRED TRAINING

1 Project management standards.

2 Technical and documentation standards.

3 Previous experience as Back-up on a project of similar
   size (or larger).

Fig. 2.12 Team Leader mission.

TEAM   Project Management Team

TEAM MEMBER   Team Leader

TASKS

1   To prepare detailed technical plans for the phase at
    the request of the Project Leader.

2   To prepare individual activity plans for the Team Members.

3   To advise the Project Leader on the quality control
    points needed.

4   To monitor the quality of the products of the phase via
    the quality control points.

5   To ensure that all Team Members are trained in the
    necessary technical standards and techniques.

6   To report regularly on project resources used.

7   To report regularly on project technical status.

8   To advise the Project Leader immediately of any
    deviation beyond tolerance levels in terms of quality
    or schedule.

9   To advise Team Members or obtain advice for them on
    all technical matters.

10 To be responsible for the sizing and assessment of
    impact of all modification requests.

Fig. 2.12 (cont.)

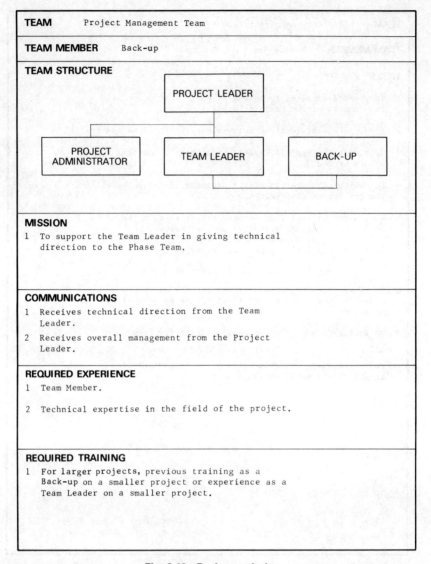

TEAM   Project Management Team

TEAM MEMBER   Back-up

TEAM STRUCTURE

MISSION

1   To support the Team Leader in giving technical
    direction to the Phase Team.

COMMUNICATIONS

1   Receives technical direction from the Team
    Leader.

2   Receives overall management from the Project
    Leader.

REQUIRED EXPERIENCE

1   Team Member.

2   Technical expertise in the field of the project.

REQUIRED TRAINING

1   For larger projects, previous training as a
    Back-up on a smaller project or experience as a
    Team Leader on a smaller project.

Fig. 2.13 Back-up mission.

TEAM	Project Management Team
TEAM MEMBER	Back-up

TASKS

1 To perform phase tasks as allocated by the
   Project Leader.

2 To assist the Team Leader as directed with the
   monitoring of technical quality.

3 To assist with the training of Team Members in
   technical standards.

4 To assist the Team Leader in technical plan
   preparation.

5 To take responsibility for the provision of any
   technical tools required by the Project
   Administrator.

6 To take responsibility for the provision of any
   technical tools required by the Phase Team.

7 To keep abreast of technical developments
   related to the project hardware and software.

Fig. 2.13 (cont.)

TEAM	Feasibility Study Phase Team

TEAM MEMBER

TEAM STRUCTURE

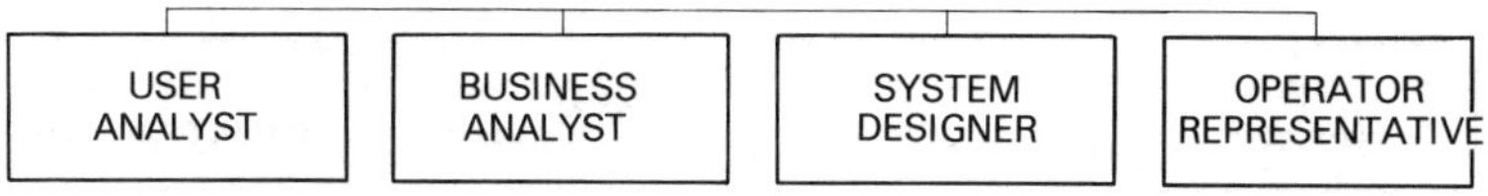

USER ANALYST	BUSINESS ANALYST	SYSTEM DESIGNER	OPERATOR REPRESENTATIVE

MISSION

1 To obtain sufficient information about the problem to enable a recommended solution and its likely cost to be put forward.

COMMUNICATIONS

1 Receives direction from the Project Leader.
2 Receives technical guidance and direction from the Team Leader.
3 Liaises with the prospective user via the User Analyst function.
4 Reports task status and resource use to the Project Administrator.

REQUIRED EXPERIENCE

REQUIRED TRAINING

Fig. 2.14 Feasibility Study Phase Team mission.

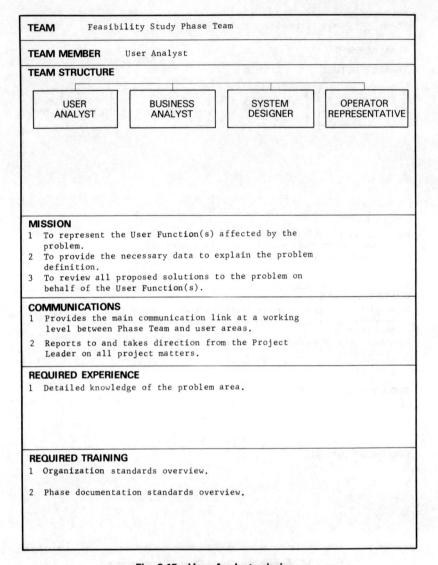

Fig. 2.15 User Analyst mission.

TEAM   Feasibility Study Phase Team

TEAM MEMBER   User Analyst

TASKS

1   To provide more explanation of the reasons for the
    project where necessary.

2   To expand the problem definition by providing more
    detail of the user problem.

3   To define acceptance criteria for measurement of
    any proposed solution.

4   To provide details of the current product(s).

5   To provide details of the operating costs
    of the current product(s).

6   To compare proposed solutions against the product
    acceptance criteria.

7   To select the most satisfactory alternative.

8   To review the problem definition in the light
    of the proposed solutions and decide if revision
    is necessary.

Fig. 2.15   (cont.)

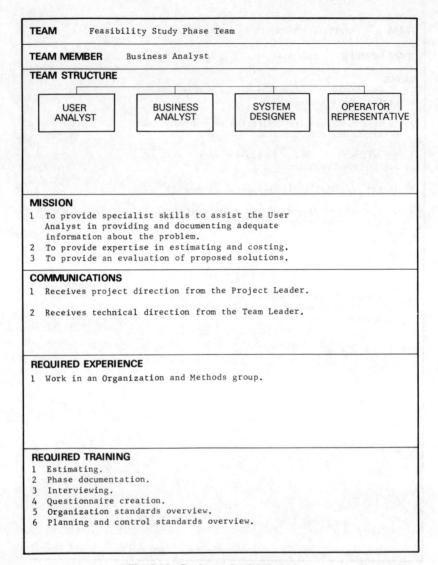

Fig. 2.16 Business Analyst mission.

TEAM Feasibility Study Phase Team

TEAM MEMBER Business Analyst

TASKS

1 To read the problem definition.

2 To identify if the terms of reference are adequate.

3 To interview the User Analyst to obtain any data necessary to expand on the problem definition.

4 To prepare a questionnaire and interview the User Analyst(s) so that they may define general acceptance criteria for a solution.

5 To check the criteria with the Operator Representative and expand where necessary.

6 To provide the documentation structure and formats, and advise the User Analyst on completing the current product description.

7 To assist the User Analyst to calculate current product operating costs where necessary.

8 To calculate and document current product maintenance costs.

9 To calculate and document development, operating and maintenance costs for each alternative solution with the help of the System Designer.

10 To produce a comparison of each alternative solution against the general acceptance criteria.

11 To produce a comparison of each alternative solution against the other solutions.

12 To assemble the feasibility report.

Fig. 2.16 (cont.)

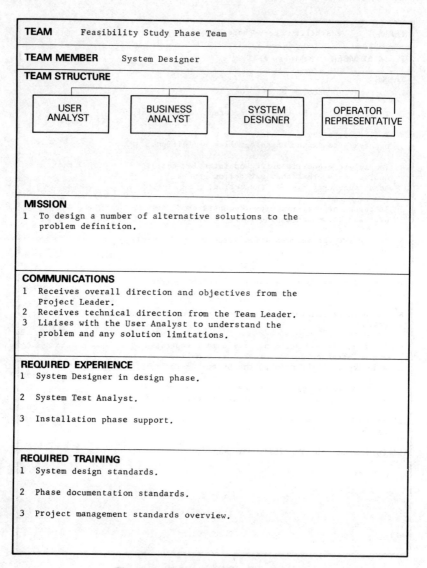

TEAM   Feasibility Study Phase Team

TEAM MEMBER   System Designer

TEAM STRUCTURE

| USER ANALYST | BUSINESS ANALYST | SYSTEM DESIGNER | OPERATOR REPRESENTATIVE |

MISSION

1   To design a number of alternative solutions to the
    problem definition.

COMMUNICATIONS

1   Receives overall direction and objectives from the
    Project Leader.
2   Receives technical direction from the Team Leader.
3   Liaises with the User Analyst to understand the
    problem and any solution limitations.

REQUIRED EXPERIENCE

1   System Designer in design phase.

2   System Test Analyst.

3   Installation phase support.

REQUIRED TRAINING

1   System design standards.

2   Phase documentation standards.

3   Project management standards overview.

Fig. 2.17   System Designer mission.

TEAM   Feasibility Study Phase Team

TEAM MEMBER   System Designer

TASKS

1 To read the problem definition.

2 To obtain clarification of the problem definition
   where necessary.

3 To understand the terms of reference of the project.

4 To understand the general acceptance criteria.

5 To document the technical description of the current
   product.

6 To design a number of alternative solutions to the
   problem.

7 To assist the Business Analyst to calculate the
   likely development costs of each proposal.

Fig. 2.17 (cont.)

TEAM Feasibility Study Phase Team

TEAM MEMBER Operator Representative

TEAM STRUCTURE

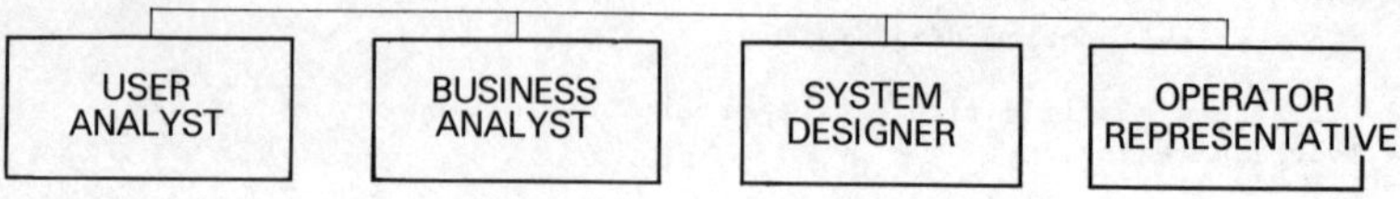
USER ANALYST
BUSINESS ANALYST
SYSTEM DESIGNER
OPERATOR REPRESENTATIVE

MISSION

1 To review the problem definition on behalf of the Operators.

2 To review proposed solutions on behalf of the Operators.

COMMUNICATIONS

1 Receives overall direction on project tasks from the Project Leader.

2 Provides communication link between project and Operators.

REQUIRED EXPERIENCE

1 Working knowledge of the operation of the current product.

2 Knowledge of the Operator facilities and environment available in the time frame to be covered by the new product development and use.

REQUIRED TRAINING

1 Project management standards overview.

2 Feasibility phase tasks.

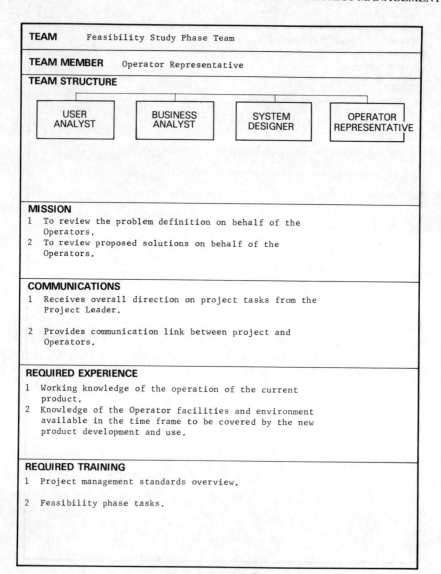

Fig. 2.18 Operator Representative mission.

TEAM   Feasibility Study Phase Team

TEAM MEMBER   Operator Representative

TASKS

1 To understand the problem definition.

2 To review the general acceptance criteria on
   behalf of the Product Operators.

3 To review the current product description on
   behalf of the Product Operators and input to
   the Business Analyst any necessary changes or
   additions.

4 To comment on each alternative solution on
   behalf of Product Operators.

Fig. 2.18   (cont.)

3 PLANNING

In this chapter, we shall examine a proposed project planning standard suitable for use with any type of planning technique.

WHY?

1 If we cannot plan a project, we will never be able to control it.
2 We need to plan a project before we can allocate individual objectives.

OBJECTIVES

1 To fit in with our team standards.
2 To fit in with our reporting.
3 To be flexible enough to allow planning for all sizes of project.
4 To permit progressive planning as more data on the project become available.
5 To permit quick recognition of any deviation from plan in actual performance.

LIMITATIONS

1 Our standard should not lead to an 'overkill' in paperwork or procedures for small projects.
2 It should fit in with a number of techniques in plan preparation, such as bar charts, networks etc.
3 Often projects are too large to be adequately planned in one step.
4 There is often insufficient information available properly to plan a project completely at the beginning.

SOLUTION

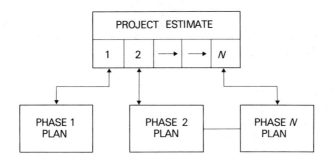

Fig. 3.1   Standard planning structure.

The solution is a standard structure as shown in Fig. 3.1.

Project estimate

This is produced during the early investigation into the feasibility of a project. There will normally be several possible solutions to the problem. In order to help decide which alternative is best, we usually need to know the comparable costs. The development cost of each possible solution must therefore be estimated. Thus, when one of the alternatives is recommended, its estimated development cost becomes the project estimate. A few points should be made about estimating.

1 It is normally done when least is known about the user's needs.
2 Nothing is known about the problems and pitfalls that will arise during the project.
3 We tend to think of a straightforward solution to the problem and forget the ancillary activities of set-up, conversion, security, human inefficiency etc.
4 Subconsciously, the person making the estimate wants to please the user or their own manager and is therefore tempted to be optimistic.
5 Estimating should be based on historical data. How long has it taken us to do comparable projects in the past? What is the effective work capacity of a Team Member during a work period? Can we learn from experiences of other Project Leaders?
6 Any estimate should show a break-down of the total project into phases. A phase is a portion of the total project duration during which certain pre-defined tasks are carried out. This will allow us to compare each phase plan with our original estimate as the project progresses.

There are a number of surveys available on the percentage of time spent in the different phases of a project. Each company should be able to develop its own average percentages according to the type of project it undertakes and its past history of projects. For those without such averages, they could start with the following figures.

Feasibility	3%
Specification	12%
Design	20%
Programming	35%
System test	15%
Installation	15%

Phase plans

Depending upon the size of the project, we must plan it in a number of discrete phases. Phases are discussed in another chapter of this book.

For each phase, we need two types of plan; a technical plan showing the tasks, resource and time allocation, and a financial plan which translates the resources into monetary terms. The technical plan is the main document for the Project Leader. The financial plan is the communicating document between Project Leader and Project Board.

Phase plans are produced prior to the start of a phase. An exception here is the plan for the very first phase which is done as one of the first tasks of that phase.

Planning package contents

A graphic plan is inadequate alone. It needs explanation to a reader. A complete planning package should consist of:

A graphic plan
A description
Assumptions on which the plan is based
Potential problems

When our schedule slips, it will be too late to say to the contractor representative 'I thought I would have priority'. If we are making such assumptions when planning, we must make this clear to those who will approve our plan.

Resource availability plan

Before creating a technical plan for a phase, it is usually worthwhile to create a schedule showing the availability of the phase resources. This covers not only the Team Members, but also the other resources required. Such a plan will include data on when each resource becomes available, when its availability ceases, and when it is not available during the phase. The availability plan also notes holidays, training and allocation to other projects, thus providing a useful check of availability against the technical plan being created.

Deviation plan

Approval and acceptance of a phase plan means certain things. The user or customer is committed to a defined level of cost, but in turn expects the project to reach a certain point for that cost by a certain date and with a certain level of quality. If one of these factors should begin to vary beyond an agreed tolerance limit, it is the responsibility of the Project Leader to bring this to the attention of the Project Board. As described in the chapter on control, this is done at a meeting with the Project Board. At this meeting, the Project Leader will present a deviation plan.

The description part of this deviation planning package describes the problem, the reason, the impact, the possible alternatives and the Project Leader's recommendation. The graphic plan will normally cover only the problem area and will extend until either the phase end or the recovery from the deviation, if this is sooner. It is not necessary for the deviation plan to go beyond the phase end. Any recovery work to be done after that will be incorporated in the next normal phase plan.

PLANNING ACTIVITIES

For those who like to approach planning in a methodical fashion, here is a general sequence of actions to follow.

Complete the provisional 'duration' and 'end date' lines. This is achieved either by copying from the final estimate, or, if a project completion date is imposed by some external factor, by calculating the stage durations by working back from the end date.

Remember that this is elapsed time, not manpower.

Complete the resources section showing how much effort is available if the size of the Phase Team is already known.

Examine the task checklists and mark any which are not applicable to the particular project.

Identify any special tasks which are not in the checklists.

Identify any necessary tasks on the checklists which have already been completed. For example, a description of the current product should normally be available.

Consider the management of the project and allocate a percentage of manpower resource for this function throughout the plan.

Identify, under applicable activities, those which can only be done by a certain Team Member.

Calculate the length of time needed for each task.

Allocate the time to produce each sub-product within the project. It is usually easiest to work backwards from the completion dates of the major tasks.

Define which activities can be done in parallel and which must be serial.

Define quality control points.

Add to the activities the time for quality control plus time for regular meetings.

Total the resources required.

Review the completed plan for individual workload balance, continuity of work for each Team Member, and re-cycle, where necessary, to smooth the workload.

Determine whether any remaining time problems are best resolved by extra resources, the purchase of external products, stretching elapsed time, or reducing the facilities to be provided by the current project.

Calculate the cost of the planned resources.

Add the tolerance percentage (either standard, or agreed with Project Board.)

Compare with the final estimate from the feasibility study.

Write the plan description to provide an explanation of the graphic plan, and how it will be implemented. This description includes information on how the plan will be monitored, and the Project Leader's proposal of a suitable tolerance level.

List the technical and business assumptions which have been made when developing the plan. It is important to document these assumptions, so that any changes to them can be quickly identified and appropriate action taken.

Identify potential problems and the likely impact on the plan should they occur.

4 CONTROL

This chapter considers the need to control various aspects of a project, and covers the control requirements of the various groups involved in a project. It also deals with the problem of written and verbal communications in a team and project environment.

WHY?

Why do we need standards for the control of a project? The correct use of control standards enables us to answer the following questions, often asked during a project.

1   What is the quality of workmanship?
2   Are we still producing what the customer wants?
3   Are we on schedule?
4   Are we within budget?
5   Will we fail to realize that schedule or budget problems have occurred until it is too late to do anything about it?
6   How are Project Board members, not normally involved with the project on a day-to-day basis, made aware of the project status?
7   When and how often should the Project Leader meet the Project Board?
8   How do we keep control of customer requests for alterations and additions after the specification and probably the cost have been agreed? How do we prevent such requests from destroying the project schedule and budget?

OBJECTIVES

1   To pass status information upwards from Team Member to Project Board.

2   To enable the Project Leader to spot deviations from budget or schedule as soon as they occur.
3   To keep the team informed.
4   To provide a standard procedure for meetings.
5   To identify the circumstances under which a meeting should be called.
6   To decide who should attend this meeting.

LIMITATIONS

1   The standards must work for large and small projects.
2   They must fit in with all our team standards.
3 · The standards must recognize that Project Board members have another day-to-day job.
4   Bureaucracy should be avoided.

SOLUTION

There are two major activities in control:

Collection of project information
Interpretation of that information to the correct people

The information is of two types:

Technical
Financial

In our solution, we shall consider two ways of interpreting the information and passing it on; the use of meetings and of reports. As far as our project management standards go, the collection of data will be considered from the bottom upwards. That is, gathering data from the working level and passing it upwards to Project Leader and Project Board.
The interested parties are

Project Board
Project Management Team
Project Team

Requirements

Consider the type of information each of the parties needs.

Project Board

The Project Board members represent user and contractor management. They are not involved (or do not wish to be involved) on a day-to-day basis. If possible, they want to manage by objectives and by exception. As management, they are mainly concerned with the status of the budget. On technical matters, they are only concerned with schedule status and knowing if the customer will get what he wants at the end of the project. They therefore do not want too much technical detail, but brief status information until things begin to go wrong. Then they need early advice of what is going wrong, together with a means of collecting all the relevant detail plus technical solution proposals.

Project Management Team

The Project Leader needs both technical and financial information regularly. The Team Leader needs up-to-date technical progress and quality information.

Phase Team

Team Members need to be able to measure their own progress against objectives, and know the status of any interfaces within the team. They need to be able to identify with the total product.

Reports

We can provide a simple recording and reporting structure to suit large and small projects. Below is a brief description of the recording and reporting activities, plus the proposed forms.

Time sheet

By: Team Members
For: Team Leader
Frequency: Daily

Team Members record efforts against tasks on time sheets. Figure 4.1 is an example of a time sheet.

WORK SHEET FOR WEEK ENDING...............

Name................

Time Units ¼ hour
(Normal Day = 6¾ hours = 27 units)

Work Typ Code		Monday				Tuesday				Wednesday				Thursday				Friday				Hash Totals
		Dept.	Proj.	Task	Time	Dept.	Proj.	Task	Time	Dept.	Proj.	Task	Time	Dept.	Proj.	Task	Time	Dept.	Proj.	Task	Time	
6	7	8		16	17	18	19		27	28	29	30		38	39	40	41		49	50	51	52	60	61	62	63	65
TO																											

Fig. 4.1 Sample time sheet.

Phase plan

By: Team Leader
For: Project Leader
Frequency: Weekly

Effort is recorded against the phase plan from the time sheets. Completed tasks and slippages are noted.

Status report

By: Project Leader
For: Project Board
Frequency: Monthly

A brief status report is sent to the Project Board on technical status and outstanding problems. Figure 4.2 is a suggested format for the status report.

1 The 'Bad News–Good News' box can be useful as a quick reference. Ticks in both centre column boxes indicate that the project is on schedule and on budget. Numbers in the right-hand column mean that the project is '$n\%$' under budget or 'n' mandays ahead of schedule. Conversely, figures in the left-hand column mean '$n\%$' over budget or 'n' mandays behind schedule.
   Under 'This Period', the major tasks completed in the past two weeks are listed; under 'Next Period', the tasks for completion in the next two weeks. 'Problems' gives the Project Leader a formal point to identify problems, and the warning signs of future budget or schedule problems. It is also a place where a note should explain why any of the tasks listed under 'Next Period' in the previous report have not appeared under 'This Period' as completions in this report.

Phase summary

By: Project Leader
For: Project Board
Frequency: Monthly

The phase summary is in graphic form to allow summarized information to be passed in a very brief document. Its main purpose is to pass

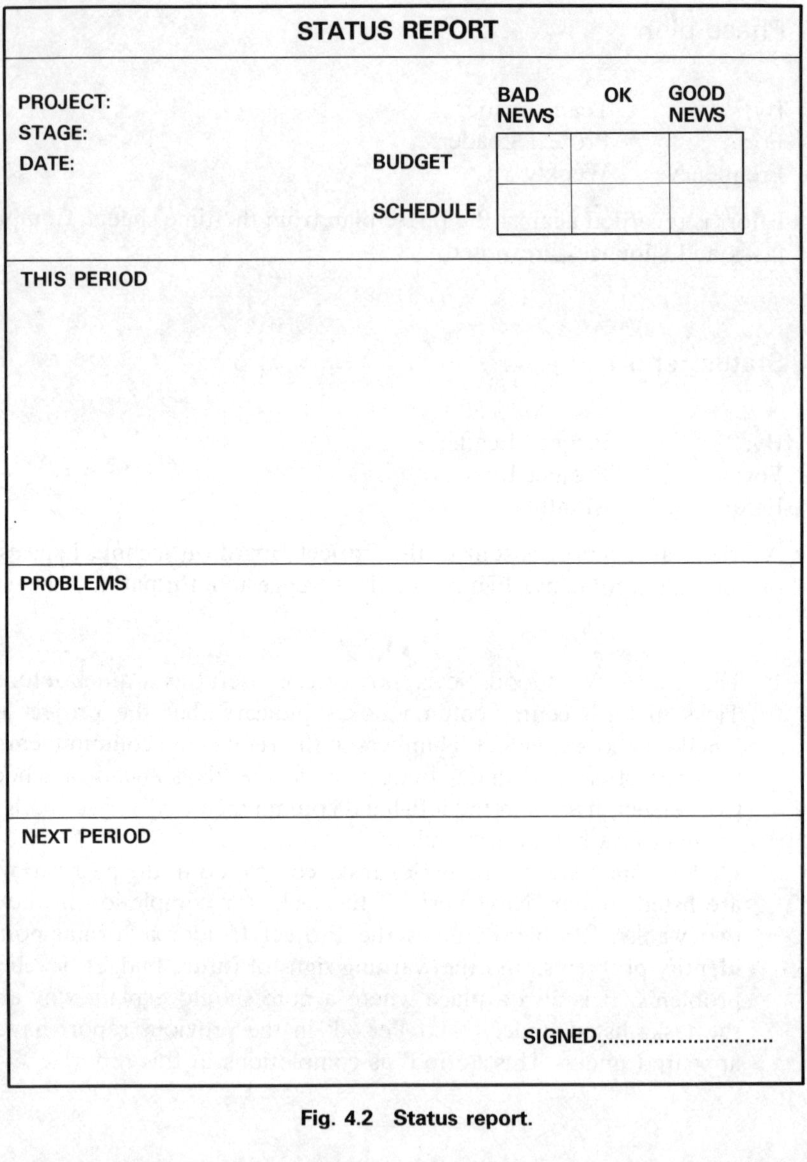

STATUS REPORT			

PROJECT:
STAGE:
DATE:

	BAD NEWS	OK	GOOD NEWS
BUDGET			
SCHEDULE			

THIS PERIOD

PROBLEMS

NEXT PERIOD

SIGNED..............................

Fig. 4.2   Status report.

financial information to the Project Board. Figure 4.3 is an example of a financial status report currently used by BP Trading, and reproduced here with their kind permission. An explanation of its completion and meaning is given below.

1   The costs of the resources consumed are recorded. A report is sent to the Project Board in graphic form, comparing current phase cumulative costs and completed tasks with the plan.

PROJECT/PHASE SUMMARY

PREPARED BY _____   PROJECT IDENTITY _____
DATE _____   PHASE _____

START	ESTIMATE			FINISH	ESTIMATE	
DATE	ACTUAL			DATE	ACTUAL	

TIME / COSTS	B/F		E	A	E	A	E	A	E	A	E	A
	E	A										
MAN DAYS												
CUMULATIVE MAN DAYS												
COMPUTER TIME												
CUMULATIVE COMPUTER TIME												
MAN DAY COST												
COMPUTER TIME COST												
OTHER COSTS												
TOTAL PERIOD COST												
TOTAL CUMULATIVE COST												
% WORK PLANNED COMPLETED												
BUDGET COMPARISON (UNDER -) (OVER +)												
SCHEDULE COMPARISON (AHEAD -) (BEHIND+)												

E = Estimate   A = Actual

Fig. 4.3 Phase summary.

2   In certain recording systems, one trap into which it is easy to fall at this time is that the team are asked to estimate 'percentage complete' for their current unfinished tasks. The danger is that this is a subjective estimate, normally optimistic, and therefore misleading. The Project Leader also has the problem of assessing all the team's estimates on different sizes of task and turning these into a single 'percentage complete' for the phase. A much better idea is the one incorporated by BP in their plan. Having produced the phase technical plan, each task in the plan is calculated as a percentage of the total phase plan. This is done by taking the total mandays needed as 100% and calculating each task's effort as a percentage of that. When reporting against the plan, completed tasks are noted and their percentage totalled to give the 'percentage complete'. In reporting

this figure, we ignore any tasks which have started but are not yet complete. In order for this approach to be really effective, no task in our plan should be greater than 10% of the total phase effort, or 10 man days for a small project. Any task larger than this can always be broken down.

3 The '% Work Planned Completed' is a cumulative figure, and is calculated by adding up the percentages of the total phase effort of those tasks which have completed so far.

Modification requests

By: Usually a user
For: Review by the Project Board
Frequency: As required

There is one other type of report which is vital if a project is to be kept under control. There must be a document produced for every major change proposed after the feasibility study, and for every major or minor change proposed after the user specification has been signed. The implementation of such changes without proper control and authority has been responsible for many project failures to meet schedule and/or budget.

Let us make this point. Having accepted the feasibility estimate, approved the user specification, and committed resources against those documents, only the Project Board has the authority to agree to any changes. Only the customer has the authority to agree to more expenditure, and this must be done at Project Board level.

The procedure should be that anyone requesting a modification should document it. The request should be assessed for its impact on the project and its likely cost. All outstanding requests should be reviewed by the Project Board at the next project review meeting. Where agreement is reached to implement certain requests, the Project Board must approve the necessary extra resources and time.

Figure 4.4 illustrates the necessary contents of a Modification Request.

Meetings

Only two types of meeting are described here; the Phase Review Meeting and the Walkthrough. The first is the formal meeting of Project Board and

MODIFICATION REQUEST	
PROJECT	M.R. NO:
REQUESTED BY:	
DESCRIPTION	
REASON & BENEFITS	
REQUIRED DATE	
TECHNICAL EVALUATION	
IMPACT ON PROJECT	
COST	
DECISION	
AUTHORIZATION	

Fig. 4.4 Modification request.

Team Leader at defined times during the project. The definition of these times relates to the size of the project, and this is covered in Chapter 5. The second is a quality control meeting. These are the types of meeting for which we must define very clear standards. There may be other types of meeting during the projects lifetime, but normally they will not require such rigorous standards.

Phase review meeting

The purposes of this meeting are as follows.
1   For the Project Board and Project Leader to meet;
2   For the Project Board to hear a more detailed report of progress and have the opportunity to ask questions;
3   For the presentation of plans to the Project Board for their approval;
4   For the Project Board to consider changes of direction (enhancements, dilutions, changes etc.) for the project;
5   For commitment of resources to the project by the Project Board;
6   To terminate the project, either at its completion, or earlier if the Project Board considers that a valid business case for the project has ceased to exist.

MANDATORY ATTENDEES

Project Board
Project Leader
Internal Auditor

OPTIONAL ATTENDEES

Appointed Technical Specialists
Team Leader
Project Administrator

MANDATORY OCCASIONS

Project start
Project termination
End of each phase
Deviation review

OPTIONAL OCCASIONS

1   Modification request review
2   Early start to next phase
3   At pre-determined intervals during a long project phase, say every 8 weeks

TASKS

1   To review the current phase.
2   To review the total project so far.
3   To review project modification requests.

4 To obtain Project Board decisions for future work.
5 To allow the Project Board to hear independent assessments of the project.

POSSIBLE AGENDA

1 Minutes of the last project review meeting.
2 Current phase plan versus actuals.
3 Total project estimate versus actuals.
4 Project Leader's status report.
5 Modification request review.
6 Internal audit report.
7 Next phase plan presentation.
8 Reappraisal of original estimate to the end of the project.

Walkthrough

This is the second type of meeting which will be useful in project control. Its main function is not the imparting of knowledge by one person to a group, but the imparting of an evaluation by a group to one person. The definition of a Walkthrough is:

a team method of checking product quality.

The major objectives of a Walkthrough are:

to improve quality by error identification,
to check any deviation from standards.

Walkthroughs can also help the Project and Team Leaders

to educate new Team Members.

It also imparts a greater degree of confidence in a task being completed if the end-product of that task has been the subject of a Walkthrough.

A Walkthrough has three parts:

Preparation
Review
Follow-up

Let us examine each of these parts in turn, looking at the objective of the part, the roles to be played in it, the documentation for that part, and finally the major activities during that part. It should be stressed that although there may be a number of roles to be taken, one person may often take several roles, especially in a small project. Most practical Walkthroughs will be carried out by two people, but it is still important for them to know how they have shared the various roles between them, so that they can check that they have fulfilled their obligations.

PREPARATION

Objective

1 To become familiar with product under review.

Roles

1 Error-finding.
2 Check for completeness.
3 Check against standards.
4 Education.

Documentation

1 Request to attend a Walkthrough.
2 Checklist of questions to ask for this type of product.
3 The piece of work to be reviewed.
4 Minor errors list.

Activities

1 Distribution of the work to be reviewed.
2 Review of the product.
3 Compilation of list of minor errors.
4 Noting points for discussion.

REVIEW

Objective

1 To review the product and produce a list of any corrections needed.

Roles

1 Chairman.
2 Secretary.
3 Reviewee.
4 Reviewer(s).

Documentation

1 Product.
2 Lists of minor errors.
3 Action list.

Activities

1 Collection of minor errors.
2 Chairman's introduction.
3 Listing of problems (no explanation at this time).
4 Step-by-step review.
   It is up to the Chairman to:
       sense concensus,

stop repetition,
take a problem off-line if no agreement can be reached,
maintain impetus.
5   Secretary notes actions.
6   Action list read-back.
7   Who will take action to correct the identified errors?
8   Who will check the corrective actions?
9   Go to follow-up or re-schedule?

Figure 4.5 is an example of a Walkthrough action list.

WALKTHROUGH ACTION LIST				
PROJECT				
PHASE				
DATE				
PRODUCT				
Action no	**Description**	**Action by**	**Target date**	**Checked by**
CHAIRMAN'S SIGN-OFF _____				

Fig. 4.5   Walkthrough action list.

FOLLOW-UP

Objectives

1 To ensure that all errors notified during the review are corrected.

Role

1 Actioner.
2 Checker.

Documentation

1 Completed action list.
2 Revised product.
3 Notification to management.

Activities

1 Resolution of errors.
2 Sign-off by nominated reviewers of the individual action items.
3 Sign-off by the Chairman at the foot of the action list, confirming that all items have been corrected and approved.
4 Notification to Project Leader.

We have now described the formal procedure for a Walkthrough. Not all Walkthroughs in a project will be formal meetings with four or more attendees. Were this the case, we should be spending far too much time and resource in Walkthroughs. To avoid this, there are a number of options open to the Project Leader and Team Leader when making their decisions on how many Walkthroughs to hold.

1 What are the key points in the project? Where are critical decisions made from where a lot of work will stem? Where is it most important to check that we are right?
2 What is known about the quality of work of the individual Team Members? Can some members be allocated just a few Walkthroughs, with more for trainees?
3 Which Walkthrough can be handled by only two people? In practice, most Walkthroughs will be of this informal type, with two people sharing the roles between them. For example, in the review, the reviewer might also take the role of chairman, leaving the reviewee to be also the secretary.

5 PHASES

In the chapters on Planning and Control, we defined a need to split a project into segments which were easier to manage. This chapter examines a method of achieving this segmentation in a standard way.

WHY?

Why do we need to think of project phases?

1 Consider these typical complaints about projects by the user.

'The end product was not what we originally asked for.'
'The project changed direction without our realizing it.'
'The cost escalated without our realizing it, and then it was too late to stop it.'
'We were in the dark during most of the development,'

In order to recognize if and when a project is going off course, there should be standard key moments in any project when all parties can review the current status of the project in terms of budget, schedule, quality and direction. The division of a project into certain blocks of achievement (phases) will define these key moments.

Several other reasons spring to mind immediately.

2 There will be times when our user wants to pause and review the situation. The division of a project into phases shows us the formal times for such reviews.
3 With larger projects, we may not be able to plan all the steps in detail at the beginning of the project. It is more accurate to plan in shorter phases.
4 If in the early part of our project we are going to consider several possible solutions, we must plan in at least two phases, the second phase starting when we decide on which alternative to choose.

5   We may know the situation over the next short period very well. The
    further into the future we look, the greater the number of unknown (and
    usually adverse) deviations there will be. If possible, therefore, we want
    to limit any firm commitment to that period ahead which is well defined
    (the next phase).
6   Trying to measure progress against a distant target date is usually mean-
    ingless. While the target remains distant, it is easy to be complacent. We
    can always recover, we tell ourselves. Panic sets in as the target date gets
    close and it becomes clear that the remaining steps need more time than
    remains. Keeping to shorter phases makes measurement and therefore
    control easier.

OBJECTIVES

We need the concept of project phases in order to answer the following
questions.

How much of this project can we plan at this time with a good chance of
completing on target?
For how long will the user be happy to let the project run without a
meeting with the contractor to examine the financial and technical progress?
How much of the total project budget is the user prepared to commit at
any time?

Therefore, our individual objectives are:

1   To divide the project into parts which can be planned in detail.
2   To allow us to plan in detail much closer to the time when we shall
    actually be doing the specific tasks.
3   To provide control points at which those working on the project can
    meet with the user and their own management to review project status.
4   To allow the user to make part payments or commitments as the project
    develops.
5   To provide a framework of phases which will apply to all types of
    project.
6   To provide a framework of phases which will assist the organization of
    the necessary skills for a project.

LIMITATIONS

1   The introduction of phases should not cause a significant increase in
    project overheads.

2 The framework of phases should be flexible enough to suit very small projects as well as very large ones.
3 We must be able to handle maintenance work within the same framework of phases as new work. We do not want to have separate standards for maintenance tasks.

SOLUTION

This pattern applies to projects which might range from a shopping expedition to producing a new computerized order entry system for a company. We can take such a pattern as the basis of our framework of phases.

Figure 5.1 shows a structure of the phases and sub-phases into which we might break a project. According to the size of a particular project, we can choose the appropriate number of phases. This would then dictate how much of the project to plan in detail at any one time, what level of detail and how many control points are needed.

If we think about all the tasks we do, big and small, we can make out a generalized pattern of work which looks like this.

Define
Prepare
Action
Review
Follow-up

Remember when looking at the structure, that only the very largest projects need to be divided up into all the phases shown. We select only the divisions appropriate to the size of each project. We shall be looking at some examples at the beginning of the next chapter to illustrate this selection. In the next chapter, we have task lists for each phase.

For the remainder of this section, we shall describe each possible phase in turn.

PROJECT

This is the total task from initial idea to its completion in real terms. Many types of project, including most data processing projects, create an end-product which will have a long working life. The maintenance of this

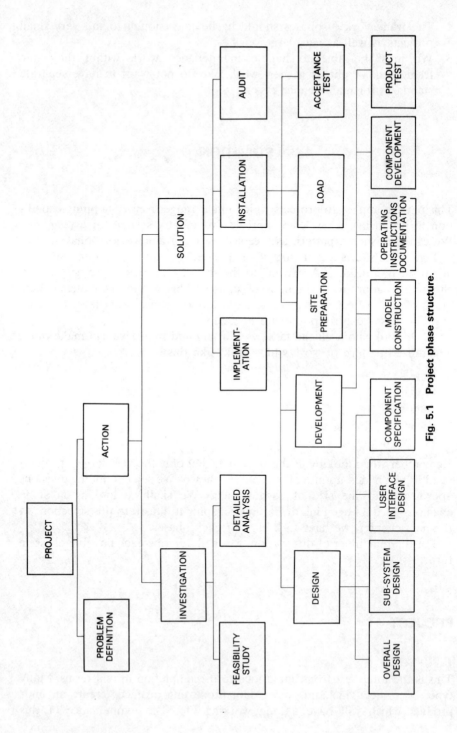

Fig. 5.1   Project phase structure.

end-product does not fall within the scope of the original project which created it. We must draw a line at the end of the original project in order to be able to measure our performance, agree final development costs with our user, and use the performance measurements to improve our estimation of future project needs. As we shall see, the maintenance and enhancement of an end-product can be handled as a series of projects.

It is not recommended that even the smallest project should be handled as a single phase. There should be at least two phases—problem definition and action—to allow an early check that we know what needs to be done, and that this is properly documented.

Problem definition

If we are to control the use of our development resources at all, all requests for use of those resources must be formally documented and authorized. The purpose of this phase, then, is both to define the problem in brief detail and to confirm that it is an authorized request.

By the end of the phase, we want to know the scope of the problem and any imposed limitations on the solution, and to have defined the management organization of the project.

There will always be a formal 'review' of a project after its problem definition. This is because we have not yet allocated any resources to look for a possible solution. There will normally be an overall group representing user and project resource managements who regularly review all problem definitions and decide to which of them resources should be allocated. Thus, there may be some 'projects' which never get beyond this phase.

There are many reasons why a problem definition may not lead to a project. It may never reach high enough on the priority list of possible projects to have resources allocated to it. There may be disagreement by management on the problem expressed. The defined problem may be overtaken by other events, incorporated into a larger problem definition, or identified as not cost effective to solve as defined.

Action

This is the overall phase in which work is done to provide a solution to the problem.

The very smallest tasks, ranging from a few manhours to perhaps as much as a man week, might be handled after the problem definition with just this phase. However, even here we should carefully check that a meeting is not needed after alternative solutions have been generated.

Although the problem defined might have been small, it does not necessarily follow that the action will be small. We may see the problem as the tip of the iceberg, needing a major effort to remedy a much larger problem, rather than a small 'patch'. What if we suggest that the solution be incorporated with other necessary work? What if the person to whom we have given this small task is inexperienced, and could decide on an alternative solution which would have disastrous effects? For these and many other reasons, we should consider carefully if another (possibly very brief) meeting is needed.

Following on from the last comment, we might wish to subdivide the 'Action' phase of a project to fit in that extra management meeting. The suggested split would be into 'Investigation' and 'Solution'.

Investigation

The phase starts with a first pass at providing (in very general terms) what the recommended solution is to be and a first estimate of the product development cost.

The main purpose of this phase is to obtain a very detailed and unambiguous specification from the user of the requirements for the product. It is essential to realize that the project contract is drawn up against this specification. Any deviation by either side from this specification later in the project must be documented and a decision made by both sides on the action to be taken.

For medium-sized projects and any project where the user is asking how much it would cost before deciding whether to go ahead with the project, investigation should be broken into two, as defined below. For the purpose of this book, we shall define a medium-sized project as one which requires between one and five man years of effort. The first phase, a feasibility study, is where we produce an estimate of how long the project will take and what resources will be needed. Even for small amounts of work there should be understanding and agreement between all involved parties on this estimate. The second part of investigation is the detailed analysis of what the user wants. Even if the project size does not warrant a Project Board meeting between feasibility and analysis, it is normally worth a check by the contractor representative.

FEASIBILITY STUDY

This is a key phase in all projects. Its purpose is to obtain sufficient information about the problem to enable a recommended solution and its likely cost to be put forward. The reason for this is to allow the user and contractor to decide whether a cost-effective case exists for carrying out the project. What is needed, therefore, is a relatively fast and inexpensive phase. In view of the decision to be made at the end of the phase, there will be a number of embryo projects which do not continue beyond this phase.

One word of warning. Although the cost estimate which is provided for the recommended solution is not intended to be a commitment, the user will continually look back to this figure during the project. Make sure that enough time is spent in assessing the likely cost. No amount of wonderful project management will rescue an over-optimistic estimate.

DETAILED ANALYSIS

The purpose of this phase is for the user to expand on the original problem definition, and specify in clear and precise detail what is expected from the finished product. This includes full details of all operations the product may be expected to perform. The user also describes how the success of the project will be measured during the installation and audit phases.

Solution

This covers the design of how we will solve the problem, the creation of the product, the tests to which we put the new product, bringing it to an operational state, and finally comparing the finished product with its original specification.
During the phase, we must watch very carefully and control any changes to the specification which was agreed at the end of Investigation. Any changes by either party must be recorded and evaluated, and a course of action agreed.
The major phases of the problem solution are Product Design, Product Development, Installation and Audit. We will group our descriptions of the other possible phases under these headings.

IMPLEMENTATION

Design

This covers the design of the overall product and any sub-products into which it might divide. It stops at the point where individual components have been identified and their functions specified. The phase also covers full consideration of how the final user will interface with the product.

Overall design   This covers the architecture of the product. Its task is to ensure that, within any imposed limitations, all required functions and outputs are met, and the necessary inputs specified. If all or part of the specification is to be met by a product which is already in existence, this is where the decision to use such a product would be made. The phase also includes definition of how the developed product is to be built and tested.

Sub-system design	This phase contains the design work for each sub-product. On very large projects, there may be several of these phases, one for each sub-product or sub-system.
User interface design	A very important part of our design work is to consider how the user will interface with and use the final product. This phase, therefore, examines the overall and sub-system design results from the point of view of the user. Will the product be easy to use? How will the user communicate with or gain access to the product? Will new tools, documents or skills be needed?
Component specification	Having designed our product down to the component level, this final part of the design lists the functions required of each component, together with any limitations and details of where each component fits in the overall product.

Development

This phase normally occupies a large percentage of any project duration. The components are designed and developed, or obtained from an existing source, tested and put together until the whole product is assembled. The operating and maintenance manuals are written. The total product is then tested against its specification and the manuals. The phase is complete when the contractor feels ready to go to the client with a finished product.

Model construction	This phase, part of Development, covers the construction of a skeleton of the final product on to which more and more detail will be hung until the final product is built. It follows the outline laid down in the Overall Design phase. In a data processing project, it would cover the construction of the basic run control statements, creation of dummy program components and data sets.
	It also gives an early impression of the final size, and permits verification of the product's communication inlets and outlets.
Operating instructions documentation	The purpose of this phase is to produce the documentation which will be needed by users, operators and maintainers of the product. Any education is also provided here. It must be done prior to the Product Test, so that tests of the documentation are included in Product Test. It is useful to do it before Component Development as it can establish standards for Component Development to use, such as naming conventions, codes and standard format.
	This phase also has the major task of reviewing the use of the final product and preparing any organization changes necessary to take full advantage of the new product.
Component development	As the name suggests, the purpose of this phase is to develop, or obtain, and test individual components for the system.
Product test	The approach of this phase is gradually to assemble the parts of the product as they are developed and test them linked together. It receives a skeleton of the system from the Model Construction phase, plus documentation and tested components from the appropriate phases. It covers the preparation of product test data

or situations and expected results. Where the preparation part of this phase may be long, the phase may start earlier than the diagram shows. It can start at any time after Design.

INSTALLATION

The purpose of this phase is to move from the point where the contractor states that a product has been produced to meet the client's specification, to the point where the client is satisfied that this is correct and is prepared to accept and use the product.

Site preparation

The purpose of this phase is to prepare the environment in which the finished product will go through its acceptance trials. With certain types of project, there may be very little to do. However, clearing a space for the product, putting in electricity or communication lines, or re-installation of necessary peripheral equipment may be necessary. For a data processing project, it will mean verifying that the identical hardware and software levels are available to those which are expected. This phase also covers any necessary training of the users.

Load

The purpose of this phase is the physical installation of the product at its destination. It includes any movement necessary from the Product Test site to the client's destination. Testing may be done at the end of loading to ensure that the product is complete and ready for Acceptance Testing.

Acceptance test

The purpose of this phase is for the client to assure himself that the product meets his original specification. The client should have prepared data or situations to simulate the possible real working conditions and test the performance, capacity and reliability of the product. Such tests should include tests of the documentation.

AUDIT

The purpose of this phase is to measure the product against the acceptance criteria given in the product specification and produce a report. It may follow immediately after the Acceptance Test phase, or there may be a time interval during which the product is actually working before the audit is done. This may depend on whether the performance of the product was required to be completely up to specification on installation or whether the contractor is expected to 'tune' the product up to the performance levels required during the first period of operational use.

6 TASKS

This chapter lists the major activities of any project, grouped under the heading of the phases discussed in Chapter 5.

WHY?

Why are task lists a useful part of our standards?

1 However experienced the Project Team is, it is always easy to forget one or two tasks.
2 A task checklist is a good aid to anyone creating a phase plan.
3 The study of the tasks will fully explain the purpose and end-products of a phase.
4 A Project Leader or Team Leader may undertake their first project without having received training in planning. It is easy to be unaware of certain tasks that should be performed.
5 Even if the Project Leader is aware of all tasks, a checklist can help by indicating the normal sequence of events.
6 Any project-oriented group should have task standards as part of their education of new leaders and as a method of emphasizing other standards to be used in the project, such as planning, reporting, monitoring and technical methods.

OBJECTIVES

1 To form a basis for any company or project to develop its own specialized task lists.
2 To act as an *aide-mémoire* to anyone planning a phase or reviewing someone else's plan.

3 To identify, together with the Phase Team descriptions, what skills are needed in the Phase Team.
4 To assist the Project Leader in allocating the tasks to individuals in the team.
5 To relate directly to the phases in Chapter 5.
6 To make it clear to which end-products within a phase each task refers.
7 To refer to other standards and techniques to be used in the project.

LIMITATIONS

1 We should be able to choose the level of detail of task list needed according to the project size.
2 The task lists should be generalized to cater for any type of project, not just data processing.
3 The tasks must relate to the project documentation standards.

SOLUTION

Each of the phases has been taken from Chapter 5 and a task list created for it. As in Chapter 5, the lists are at different levels, according to the number of phases chosen. A copy of the phase structure (Fig. 6.1) is included here to act as a reference guide.

For example, with a very small project the following phases might be chosen.

Problem Definition
Investigation
Solution

For a project of this type, the corresponding three task lists should be adequate.

With a larger, more complex project, there may be the need, for example, to break down solution into

Problem Definition
Feasibility Study
Detailed Analysis
Design
Development
Product Test
Installation
Audit

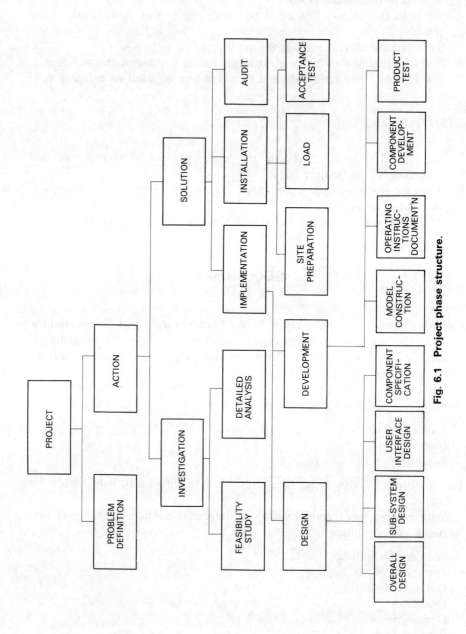

Fig. 6.1 Project phase structure.

and thus utilize the more detailed task lists. The choice of the level of detail of task list needed does not imply any increase in the time which the project will take. The use of task lists will, if anything, reduce the time taken for the project by avoiding omissions and the attendant extra time always needed to recover from them.

The naming and numbering of the task lists which follow relate them to the phase structure given in Chapter 5.

PROBLEM DEFINITION

1 Identify the problem author.
2 Describe the problem.
3 Explain briefly why a solution is being sought.
4 Define the general objectives of the solution.
5 Provide brief details of any limitations.
6 Give examples of the problem.
7 Obtain authority for the problem definition.
8 Log the request. (Add it to the list of problem definitions to be considered for resource allocation. This will normally include giving it a reference number. There may be different logs to separate new projects, enhancements and error reports.)
9 Review the problem definition as a basis for a possible project.
10 Identify the Project Board for an approved project.
11 Define the phases to be used in the project.
12 Identify the Project Leader.
13 Plan the first phase.
14 Hold a project initiation meeting.

ACTION

Investigation

1 Review problem definition.
2 Survey the current system.
3 Analyse the user needs in detail.
4 Define the product acceptance criteria.

5   Refine the project terms of reference.
6   Consider alternative solutions.
7   Evaluate each proposed solution against the acceptance criteria and terms of reference.
8   Compare alternative solutions.
9   Select the most satisfactory proposal.
10 Obtain user agreement to the recommended solution.
11 Obtain user's signed agreement to the specification of needs.

Investigation may need to be broken down into the following phases.

Feasibility study

PREPARATION

1   Read the problem definition.
2   Expand the terms of reference of the project.
3   Establish who will provide more detail of the problem.
4   Expand the reasons given for the project in the problem definition.
5   Expand the problem definition by gathering more detail of the required objectives and functions of the new product.
6   Make a first pass at defining the acceptance criteria for the new product.

CURRENT PRODUCT SURVEY

1   Survey and document the current product(s) to be replaced by the new product.
2   Identify the current product(s) running costs.
3   Identify current product(s) maintenance costs.

ALTERNATIVE SOLUTION

For each alternative solution:

1   Make a first pass at designing a product to solve the problem.
2   Establish what the external interfaces of the solution will be.
3   Calculate the development costs.
4   Calculate the running costs.
5   Identify and quantify the benefit to be gained.
6   Define the break-even point.
7   Compare with the product acceptance criteria.
8   Compare with the project's terms of reference.

RECOMMENDATION

1   Compare solutions and select the most satisfactory.
2   Review the problem definition and decide if it needs revision.
3   Prepare a feasibility report.

Detailed analysis

PRODUCT SPECIFICATION

1 Expand the problem definition to give a full description of each function of the new product.
2 Describe, as fully as possible, the required outputs of the product, providing samples if they currently exist.
3 Describe as fully as possible the required inputs to produce these outputs, providing samples if they currently exist.
4 Define precisely any special rules to be applied to produce each output.
5 Define precisely any special rules to be applied to verify each input.
6 Define the required timings for each output.
7 Define the required timings for each input.
8 Forecast the expected average and maximum volumes for each input and output.
9 Describe any likely future enhancements.

OPERATIONAL ENVIRONMENT

1 Describe the location(s) in which the product is to be used.
2 Define the maximum tolerances within which the product is expected to work in its operational environment(s).
3 Define any equipment or components which must be used.
4 Define security requirements in use of the product.
5 Define any audit data.

ACCEPTANCE CRITERIA

1 Define the required performance of the new product.
2 Define the expected reliability of the new product.
3 Define the required availability of the new product.
4 Define any standards with which the product and its documents must comply.
5 Define the types of acceptance tests to be run.
6 Define the situations which should be tested for each type of acceptance test to be run.
7 Define the maximum running costs of the product.

PROJECT TERMS OF REFERENCE

1 Define the required installation schedule.
2 Define the project cost limits.
3 Define the project status reporting requirements.

Solution

In a small project, 'Solution' picks up the result of 'Investigation', produces the answer and implements it.

1   Design the product.
2   Decide how to test the product.
3   Write the product manuals.
4   Develop the product.
5   Test the product.
6   Prepare the site.
7   Load the product.
8   Carry out acceptance tests.
9   Cut over to the new product.
10 'Tune' the new product.
11 Audit the new product against the user's specification.

In a larger project, 'Solution' may need to be sub-divided into 'Implementation', 'Installation', and 'Audit'. These are shown below, together with their sub-divisions.

Implementation

1   Design the product.
2   Design the user procedures.
3   Specify the components.
4   Define how the project will be installed.
5   Build a skeleton of the product.
6   Write the user manual.
7   Develop the components.
8   Write the maintenance manual.
9   Test the product.

Implementation is sub-divided into 'Design' and 'Development'.

DESIGN

Overall design
1   Understand the detailed analysis.
2   Review the recommended solution design against the finalized user requirements.
3   Evaluate and report on any modification necessary to make the outline solution fit the user requirements.
4   Review the revised outline against the project terms of reference where necessary, and advise the user of any changes.
5   Describe the product build and test environment, and highlight any differences to the operational environment.
6   Ensure that each output is produced in the product design.
7   Ensure that the required input is made available in the design.
8   Identify any additional input required.

9   Check for ancillary functions needed in the design for product set-up and modification during operation.
10 Design how any audit requirements will be met.
11 Identify the sub-systems into which the product will be broken for development.
12 Design the interface between the sub-systems.
13 Verify that the design will meet the volume requirements for each input and output.
14 Verify that the design will meet the timing requirements for each input and output.
15 Verify that there is no disparity between required outputs and available inputs.
16 Verify that the design will meet the standards defined in the detailed analysis.
17 Verify that the design will use the components defined in the detailed analysis.

Installation strategy	1	Compare the desired installation schedule defined by the user with overall product design.
	2	Define how the product will be installed.
	3	Define how the product installation will be tested.
	4	Specify the installation test data or situations.
Development strategy	1	Decide into how many sub-systems the product will be divided for development.
	2	Allocate a sequence to the construction of the sub-systems, bearing the installation strategy in mind.
	3	Identify any test devices required.
Product test strategy	1	Understand the detailed analysis.
	2	Plan the test cases needed in the product test.
	3	Create the test cases.
	4	Identify any test devices required.
Acceptance strategy	1	Understand the installation strategy.
	2	Understand the acceptance criteria.
	3	Identify all parties to be involved in acceptance tests.
	4	Plan how the acceptance tests are to be carried out.
	5	Allocate acceptance test responsibilities.
	6	Review the acceptance test strategy with all those involved and obtain agreement.

Sub-system design

1 Understand the overall design.
2 Understand from the detailed analysis the functions to be performed by the sub-system.
3 Understand the inter-sub-system interfaces.
4 Define (or confirm) the media to be used for all interfaces.
5 Design the external and inter-sub-system interface layouts in detail.
6 Design the internal structure, functions and paths between interfaces down to component level.
7 Identify and design any extra ancillary functions needed.
8 Define the media and layout of any intra-sub-system interfaces.
9 Ensure the design meets the requirements specified in the operation environment and acceptance criteria.
10 Ensure the design meets the timing and volume requirements.
11 Define the sub-system responsibilities.
12 Define the sub-system test cases.

User interface design

Organization design	1	Understand the organization(s) supporting the current product(s).
	2	Understand all data paths through the current system(s) and current responsibilities.
	3	Understand the overall design of the new product.
	4	Determine all users of the new product.
	5	Establish who will have overall responsibility for the new product during its operational life.
	6	Define the decision points which will arise in the new product for abnormal conditions which may occur during its use.
	7	Identify responsibility for all decision points.
	8	Plot the data paths through the new product.
	9	Design any necessary organization changes to adapt to the new product.
	10	Establish the schedule for the organization changes.
Procedure design	1	Review the organization design document.
	2	Compare the planned data paths through the new product with those of the current product(s).
	3	Identify requirements for changes to existing procedures and for new procedures.
	4	Design new procedures and procedure changes.
	5	Identify documents needed by these procedures.
External interface design	1	Define products which interface with the existing product(s) to be replaced.
	2	Determine whether there are extra products which will interface with the new product.
	3	Ascertain the timing of the interface of these products.
	4	Identify any required changes to these products on the introduction of the new product.
	5	Produce a schedule for the required target dates for the required changes.
Training	1	Review any planned organization changes.
	2	Define the groups to be trained and the type(s) of training required.
	3	Specify each course's objectives, content and skeleton timetable.
	4	Obtain approval for the planned training.
Document design	1	Identify all interface documents to be used by the product.
	2	Establish the media of all these documents.
	3	Establish the source and destination of each document and its distribution.
	4	Define the frequencies of use of each document.
	5	Define the volume of each document.
	6	Design the layout and content of each document.

Component specification

1 Illustrate the component's place in the sub-system or product.
2 Provide full details of each output.
3 Provide full details of each input.

4   Specify functions to be carried out by component.
5   Examine each part of each input and ensure that all special rules have been detailed.
6   Identify any size or performance criteria.
7   Identify any standards or standard parts to be used.
8   Specify any required test situations.

DEVELOPMENT

1   Construct a skeleton model of the product.
2   Test the model.
3   Design all product external interface documents.
4   Write the user manual.
5   Write the installation document.
6   Prepare any necessary training.
7   Develop the individual product components.
8   Test the assembled product.

Model construction

1   Understand the product's overall design document.
2   Map out the product skeleton.
3   Understand, where applicable, the sub-system design documents.
4   Review the component specifications for likely final size and form.
5   Define the likely final product size based on the assumptions so far.
6   Ensure that the product will meet with any size criteria given in the product specification.
7   Ensure that the product will fit in its test environment.
8   Ensure that the product can be moved to its operational environment.
9   Ensure that the product will fit in its operational environment.
10 Define any techniques necessary for component development for reasons of size, speed, standardization or other significant factors.
11 Construct the product skeleton.
12 Fit empty 'shells' of the components into the skeleton.
13 Review inter-component and inter-sub-system links.
14 Review intra-product use of common components.
15 Review the inputs and outputs to the product and the ability of the model to meet their needs.
16 Refine the model if problems are discovered and update the documentation of the modified part(s) to reflect the change made.
17 Prepare model test data.
18 Test all paths through the model.
19 Modify as required and re-cycle the tests.

Operating instructions documentation

User manual   1   Write a product overview from the reader's point of view.
                     2   Write a description of each separate function of the product, including any operating rules.

                     For each function:

                     3   Define when, or the circumstances under which, each function of the product is to be used.

4 Identify the inputs, their source and the input arrangements.
5 Define the prerequisites.
6 Describe the sequence of events and expected results of each step.
7 Identify the outputs, destinations and distribution arrangements.
8 Identify the contact in case of problems and how to communicate.
9 List all possible errors.
10 Explain how to recognize each type of error when using the product.
11 Explain what steps to take after each type of error.
12 Explain how to close down the product after use.

Operator manual
If the user operates the product in question by using a third party, a more technical user's manual may be needed. An example of this is a computer with a number of users, each of them remote from the machine. There are a number of operators at the machine site to ensure that each user's differing needs are met and to keep the machine running. This group also needs documentation to understand what it has to do. The tasks to provide this documentation are exactly the same as for the user manual, but this time with a different reader in mind.

Installation package
1 Provide a bill of material of the installation package.
2 Describe the operational environment necessary.
3 Define the required installation equipment.
4 Write installation instructions.
5 Create installation tests.
6 Write installation test instructions.
7 List possible installation errors.
8 Explain each possible error and the recovery steps to take.

Training
1 Review the training strategy.
2 Create the training material and any training aids needed.
3 Produce a training schedule.

Product test

1 Review the product test strategy document.
2 Set up the product test environment to reflect the anticipated operational environment as closely as possible.
3 Identify any parts of the product operational environment which cannot be simulated.
4 Revise the test strategy document to incorporate ways of testing these parts.
5 Prepare data or situations to implement the product test strategy.
6 Ensure that all necessary user and maintenance documentation is available, and that tests of this documentation are included in product test.
7 Carry out the product test.
8 Liaise with the development group to correct any errors.
9 Re-cycle the product test and corrections until satisfied that the product is error free and meets its design document.

Product installation package
1 Prepare a bill of material for the product.
2 Ensure the installation document is available.
3 Carry out a test installation of the product working from the installation manual.

4   Test the new installation to ensure that it is complete.
5   Revise the installation manual and bill of material, if necessary.
6   Assemble the product for despatch to the user.

Installation

This is the second major part of the 'Solution'.

1   Carry out any necessary training.
2   Make any necessary organizational changes.
3   Review the differences between the product test environment and the product operational environment.
4   Prepare the product operational site.
5   Ensure that all documents required in the use of the product are available.
6   Load the product.
7   Test the product against its installation test documents.
8   Run the acceptance test(s).
9   Adjust the product as required.
10 Ensure recovery to the old product is available and secure.
11 Perform the necessary conversion tasks.
12 Cut-over to the new product.

Installation can be broken down into 'Site Preparation', 'Load' and 'Acceptance Test'.

SITE PREPARATION

People preparation

1   Make a list of all people to be affected by the new product.
2   Plan the necessary people changes for the new product.
3   Plan the necessary training.
4   Recruit any new staff necessary for the new product.
5   Carry out preliminary training.
6   Review procedure changes.
7   Review and revise the training material.
8   Carry out final training.

Site preparation

1   Confirm the site requirements.
2   Prepare the site according to requirements.
3   Define the timetable for the installation.
4   Determine the resources needed for the installation.
5   Plan the load phase and obtain the necessary agreements to resource availability and timing.

Interface preparation

1 Review new product interfaces.
2 Verify the new product interfaces with the organization changes planned, and make any necessary adjustments.
3 Prepare new interface procedures and ensure that they are compatible with new product internal procedure changes.
4 Review the steps needed for conversion from the old to the new product.
5 Prepare conversion procedures.
6 Review the steps needed to fall back to the old product if there are difficulties on cut-over to the new product.

Acceptance test preparation

1 Review on the acceptance test strategy document.
2 Decide on the types of test needed.
3 Identify acceptance test resources.
4 Allocate responsibilities and have test data prepared.
5 Document the expected results.
6 Verify the acceptance tests against the user's acceptance criteria and rectify any deviations or omissions.
7 Plan the acceptance test phase.

Load preparation

1 Read the loading instructions.
2 Assemble all the items needed.
3 Perform security tasks to ensure recovery from any loading failures.

LOAD

1 Load the product.
2 Run tests to ensure that all parts of the product are present and assembled.
3 Check test results.
4 Develop action plan and schedule to resolve loading problems.
5 Adjust the product, reset the environment and re-cycle the load and test.
6 Carry out any further tasks defined in the loading instructions.
7 Test that the product interfaces with its operational environment.

ACCEPTANCE TEST

1 Study the acceptance criteria and acceptance test strategy.
2 Prepare tests and expected results for the applicable types of test from the following list.

> Function Test
> Volume Test
> Performance Test
> Interface Test
> Reliability Test
> Documentation Test
> Error Recovery Test

       Fall-back Test
       Procedure Test
       Operator Test
       Organization Test
       Destruction Test

3 Run the acceptance tests.
4 Check the results.
5 Identify problems.
6 Develop an action list and schedule for problem solution.
7 Make the necessary adjustments.
8 Re-cycle through the acceptance tests until satisfactory results produced.
9 Produce a report.

Audit

This is the final phase of 'Solution' and looks back at the job which has been done.

PRODUCT AUDIT

1 Obtain the acceptance criteria from the detailed analysis.
2 Examine the list of errors discovered since installation and compare this with the reliability factor demanded by the user.
3 Obtain details of the total operational time of the product.
4 Calculate MTBF (Mean Time Between Failures) from the total operational time divided by the number of serious errors, and compare this with the acceptance criterion.
5 From the error records, calculate the MTTR (Mean Time To Repair) and compare this with its acceptance criterion.
6 From the error records, calculate the maintenance costs and forecast the likely average maintenance costs for comparison with the acceptance criterion.
7 Verify the use and correct function of control procedures covering error reporting, enhancement requesting, making modifications, testing and updating the product.
8 Set up and run tests to obtain performance statistics.
9 Compare the performance statistics with the acceptance criteria and identify areas needing improvement.
10 Create a test environment and modify the product according to the required improvements.
11 Monitor performance of test environment.
12 Re-cycle product adjustment and tests until the performance criteria are met.
13 Assess operating costs and compare with acceptance criterion.
14 Interview users and maintainers on the accuracy and adequacy of the documentation.
15 Verify that the fall-back procedures and equipment are being maintained and are operable.
16 Write a report on the comparison of the product with its acceptance criteria.

PROJECT AUDIT

1 Record the final actuals on the last phase plan and the project plan.
2 Compare the actual resource usage with the plan for both the final phase and the total project, and calculate the deviations.
3 Document, where necessary, any reasons for deviation in the final phase, including assumptions which were not fulfilled.
4 Record project statistics to improve future project estimation.

7 DOCUMENTATION

This chapter identifies the need for documentation standards for any project, and proposes a documentation structure, with a number of examples of specific form layouts.

WHY?

1 Before repair or improvement work can be carried out, one often experiences difficulty in finding where the system developers recorded what they did, why they did it, and how they did it.
2 Most projects produce an end-product which needs instructions on its use.
3 Poor instructions on the use of an end-product can seriously affect the acceptability of the product.
4 Verbal transfer of information between users and developers is prone to the human failings of misunderstanding and forgetfulness.
5 Without documentation, there is no audit trail through the project work.
6 Documentation means commitment.
7 Many developers hate having to document.

OBJECTIVES

1 To cover the transfer of technical and business information.
2 To provide a comprehensive record of customer/user requirements.
3 To show how the end-product will be evaluated for success.
4 To record how the developer designs and creates an end-product to meet the user requirements.
5 To be capable of recording any changes to requirements.

LIMITATIONS

1   On small projects, the standards should not cause an unnecessary paperwork load.
2   The standards should avoid duplication.
3   Completion of the various parts of a documentation must fit in with the phase tasks and be measurable at a phase end.

SOLUTION

Business documentation

One of the objectives is that documentation should cover both technical and business documentation. Business documentation has, in fact, been covered in the chapter on control. To summarize, business documentation consists of:

Plans
Reports
End-phase signed agreements
Walkthrough documentation
Modification requests

Together these form a business audit trail through the project covering project objectives (and any changes to them), the intended steps to meet these objectives, commitments to dates, costs and resources, the quality of the steps, and finally the performance against the commitments.

Technical documentation

Many companies do not have documentation standards. Many development team members dislike having to document what they have done. Sometimes this is because they cannot see the purpose of the document they are producing. Often it is because the company standards are poor or inflexible, and the staff feel that they are writing because it is imposed in the standards, and that their work will never be read. People always hate having to document after the event. There is no personal motivation to do this. On the other hand, people do see the sense in documenting what they want someone else to do for them, and they see the benefit in documentation which helps them formulate their ideas and design solutions. If we can put all these good and bad points together, we should be able to produce a standard to satisfy them and meet the objectives of this chapter.

The first point, then is:

documentation is for the reader.

If we cannot identify the reader, we do not write the document. Having identified the reader, what does the reader want to read, and what documentation will only get in the way? How much information does the reader want? The reader, of course, may also be the writer, if it is part of the solution documentation. The second point is that we shall either document in advance or concurrently with the task in question. We shall never document after the event. This has significant impact on when we write the user manual, installation manual, testing and maintenance documentation.

Documentation structure

Here is an index for our documentation structure.

Volume 1   Project Overview

      Chapter 1   Terms of Reference
      Chapter 2   Project Scope
      Chapter 3   Project Organization
      Chapter 4   Summary of Recommendation
      Chapter 5   Current Status

Volume 2   Current System

      Chapter 1   System Description
      Chapter 2   System Structure
      Chapter 3   Organization
      Chapter 4   Outputs
      Chapter 5   Inputs
      Chapter 6   Internal Files
      Chapter 7   Development Costs
      Chapter 8   Maintenance Costs
      Chapter 9   Operating Costs
      Chapter 10   Evaluation

Volume 3   New System

Chapter 1   System Description
Chapter 2   System Structure
Chapter 3   Organization
Chapter 4   Outputs
Chapter 5   Inputs
Chapter 6   Internal Files
Chapter 7   Development Costs
Chapter 8   Maintenance Costs
Chapter 9   Operating Costs
Chapter 10 Evaluation

Volume 4   Test Documents

Chapter 1   Acceptance Criteria
Chapter 2   Unit Test
Chapter 3   System Test
Chapter 4   Installation Test
Chapter 5   Acceptance Test

Volume 5   User Manual

Chapter 1   System Description
Chapter 2   Schedule
Chapter 3   Function Steps
Chapter 4   Error Messages and Recovery
Chapter 5   Glossary of Terms

Volume 6   Installation Manual

Chapter 1   Prerequisites
Chapter 2   Bill of Material
Chapter 3   Installation Steps
Chapter 4   Installation Test Steps
Chapter 5   Customization Steps

Documentation detail

This portion of the chapter looks at each chapter in turn. Where necessary, a further breakdown of headings and an explanation of the expected content are given. Production of each part of the documentation is related to the phase or phases during which it should be produced or updated. Where a volume or chapter is not needed for a project, 'not applicable' should be entered. Where an entire volume is not needed, the volume is 'not applicable'. We do not need to repeat this phrase for every chapter within that volume.

From the index, the reader may be worried about the apparent omission of certain documents normally present in project documentation. Where are the volumes for user specifications, training, maintenance, feasibility and design? Data processing people will be looking for program documentation. The ideas of this structure are to avoid duplication; to avoid re-writing the same information in another format; to provide documents which are both working documents and a historical record of project progress; and to allow development of the document in a top-down manner which parallels the development of the product.

A key concept in this structure is that a piece of information will always be in the same place. We may refine it several times during the project, which is normal, but it will always have the same reference. For example, the user begins to define his needs in general terms during the feasibility phase and will provide more detail during user specification. We should not document these in two different places.

Volume 1   Project Overview

Chapter 1   Terms of Reference

When?   At the beginning of the project.

What?   Who asked whom to undertake the project?
                 Aim of the project.
                 Reasons why the project is being undertaken.
                 Cost or resource constraints.
                 Target dates.
                 Reporting requirements.

Chapter 2   Project Scope

When?   Created prior to the start of a project as the 'trigger' to possible investigation. Clarified by the Project Leader at the beginning of the feasibility study and again at the beginning of user specification.

What?   Brief statement of the major facilities being sought. The layout shown in Fig. 7.2 should be partially filled in for this purpose.

Chapter 3   Project Organization

When?   As one of the first tasks in the project for the Project Leader.

What?   Composition of the Project Board.
                         Project Leader.
                         External interfaces.

Chapter 4   Summary of Recommendation

When?   At the end of the feasibility phase, when one alternative solution has
                         been chosen by the feasibility team.

What?   Identification of the alternative recommended and reasons.
                         Estimated total cost.
                         Estimated completion date.

Chapter 5   Current Status

When?   At the end of each phase.

What?   Which phase the project is in.
                         When the phase began.
                         Comparison with estimated project budget at that time.
                         Comparison with estimated schedule at that time.

Volume 2   Current System

Chapter 1   System Description

When?   Created during feasibility.

What?   A brief narrative description.

Chapter 2   System Structure

When?   Feasibility.

What?   A flowchart, blueprint or other graphic picture of the current system.
                         Data flow (where applicable) of inputs and outputs through the
                         system.

Chapter 3   Organization

When?   Feasibility.

What?   Current user organization structure.

Chapter 4   Outputs

When?   Feasibility

What?   Formal layout, such as Fig. 7.1, defining the content, distribution, frequency, volumes and computation concerned with each output. Notes relating to the source, calculations, inter-dependencies of output items are put behind each layout with a cross-reference in the 'notes' column of the layout.
Example of the output.

Chapter 5   Inputs

When?   Feasibility.

What?   Formal layout, such as Fig. 7.1, defining the content, source, frequency, volumes and validation concerned with each input.
Notes relating to the fields are put behind each layout with a cross-reference in the 'notes' column of the layout.

Chapter 6   Internal Files

When?   Feasibility.

What?   Formal layout, such as Fig. 7.1, defining content, frequency, volumes.
Notes relating to the fields are put behind each layout with a cross-reference in the 'notes' column of the layout.
Example of the input.

Chapter 7   Development Costs

When?   Feasibility.

What?   If applicable, the estimated cost of developing the current system to the level of the new needs.

Chapter 8   Maintenance Costs

When?   Feasibility.

What?   Costs of repairing, or providing a maintenance service for the product.

DOCUMENT ANALYSIS		
DOCUMENT NAME	REFERENCE	DATE
PURPOSE		
SOURCE/DESTINATION	MEDIUM	RETENTION PERIOD
FREQUENCY	TIME	TIME OF MAX VOL
VOLUME: MAX	AVERAGE	GROWTH

DATA FLOW

To	Action taken	Turn-round

ANALYSIS OF ELEMENTS

Element name	Type	Range		Description	Source	X-Ref
		Min	Max			

Fig. 7.1 Data description.

Chapter 9   Operating Costs

When?   Feasibility.

What?   Cost of human resources and materials in operating the current system.
Costs or loss of income caused by the failings or omissions in the current system.

EVALUATION FORM								
M = Mandatory			Score = Value × Priority					
ITEM	DESCRIPTION	MEASURE	REQUIREMENT			ALTERNATIVE X-REF		
			M	Pr'y	Value	M	Value	Score

Fig. 7.2   Project scope.

Chapter 10   Evaluation

When?   In feasibility, when all alternatives have been developed up to the
                 end of Chapter 9.

What?   A possible format is shown in Fig. 7.2
                 Comparison of the current system with the acceptance criteria for
                 the new needs.
                 If applicable, a break-even chart showing when development costs
                 would be recovered.

Volume 3   New System

This volume is a combination of the old idea of user specification with
system design. In practice, the two are developed hand-in-hand. It will
start as a one-level brief document during feasibility. As more detail is
added in specification or design, a tree structure is adopted to suit the
complexity of the system. Figure 7.3 is an example of the way Chapter 1
might develop.

A different Volume 3 will be created in feasibility for each alternative
solution. Once the choice has been made, only the Volume 3 for the
selected alternative will be refined.

Feasibility would only be concerned with putting some information in a

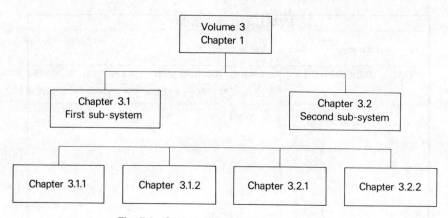

Fig. 7.3   System description tree structure

general description at the first level. User specification might expand that to give greater detail divided into two sub-systems. In design, these might be further refined to the next level to add details of how the need is to be met and to allocate needs to a part of the solution.

Chapter 1   System Description

When?   Begun during feasibility as an overview with just enough detail to
                          facilitate the examination of alternatives.
                          Refined by the user during user specification to show full detail of his
                          needs.
                          Allocated to different parts of the solution during design and im-
                          plementation with added technical detail to show how the need is to
                          be met.

What?   Same as described in Volume 2, Chapter 1.

Chapter 2   System Structure

When?   Drawn in rough outline during feasibility, expanded during design,
                          and completed during development.

What?   Same as Volume 2, Chapter 2.

Chapter 3   Organization

When?   Defined briefly in the examination of the alternative during feasibility.
                          Refined only for the selected alternative during design.

| What? | Same as Volume 2, Chapter 3. |

Chapter 4   Outputs

| When? | Started during feasibility for the major outputs.
Refined during user specification. |
| What? | Same as Volume 2, Chapter 4. |

Chapter 5   Inputs

| When? | Started during feasibility with only enough detail to permit development of alternatives.
Clarified during user specification and possibly revised during design. |
| What? | Same as Volume 2, Chapter 5. |

Chapter 6   Internal Files

| When? | Design and development. |
| What? | Same as Volume 2, Chapter 6. |

Chapter 7   Development Costs

| When? | Feasibility. |
| What? | Estimated costs of developing the alternative. |

Chapter 8   Maintenance Costs

| When? | Feasibility. |
| What? | Estimated maintenance costs of the alternative. |

Chapter 9   Operating Costs

| When? | Feasibility. |
| What? | Estimated operating costs of the alternative over, say, either a 3 or 5 year period.
Estimated loss of income associated with the alternative. |

Chapter 10   Evaluation

When?   At the end of feasibility.

What?   Formal layout, such as Fig. 7.2, comparing the alternative with the
                     user needs.
                     Each facility is given a score, according to the alternative solution's
                     ability to provide it.
                     At the end of the evaluation, each score is multiplied by its weighting
                     and a total calculated. This is to give a crude measure of which
                     alternative appears to meet the specification and acceptance criteria
                     most closely. It is not intended to be the only measure used, but it
                     does give a very clear picture, and at the very least forces the analyst
                     to evaluate very carefully the correct order of priority of needs.

Volume 4   Test Documents

There are two schools of thought on where to put test documents. One
says keep them with the subject they are testing, the other says keep all
test documents together. This book has gone for the second choice. This
makes it easier to check up on the state of testing and its quality, and
lends itself to the allocation of the tasks of supervising all testing and being
responsible for test tools, techniques and data to one Team Member or
specialist.

Chapter 1   Acceptance Criteria

When?   Begun during feasibility.
                     Refined and finalized during user specification.

What?   Figure 7.4 is an example of the information needed in a document of
                     acceptance criteria.

REF.	ACCEPTANCE CRITERIA	MEASURABLE		CALCULATION TO BE USED FOR MEASUREMENT	TARGET DATES & PERCENTAGE ACHIEVEMENT						
		Yes	No								

Fig. 7.4 Acceptance criteria.

The reference is of any type which will enable you to cross-refer to it from other documents.

Under 'Acceptance Criteria', comes a brief description of the item to be measured. Examples might be 'Response time', 'Reliability', and 'Ease of use'.

'Measurable' simply defines whether the criterion is capable of being measured in terms of how close the solution comes to meeting it. Most criteria can be measured. Measurement may be in terms of time, volume, money (saved or wasted), numbers of errors, manpower required etc.

In the column 'Calculation to be used', we define the standard to be met. For example, the criterion 'Response time' might give a calculation of five seconds average with four simultaneous users.

Once they have been installed, most systems require tuning in order to obtain the best performance. In most cases, it is unreasonable to expect performance to be refined during testing. The next six columns on the form allow for a gradual tuning of the system once installed. For example, if response time is our criterion once again, we could state here that we are prepared to accept the system at cut-over time with a response time of ten seconds. This is put in the first two columns. In the next two, we indicate that the response time must be down to, say, seven seconds within two months. In the last two columns, we indicate a final target date to achieve the original acceptance criterion of five seconds.

Chapter 2   Unit Test

When?   In the early stages of development, as a pre-requisite to component development.

What?   Figure 7.5 is an example of a format and content of a unit test document.

Under 'Control Points', the Team Leader would specify when the person appointed to the unit test should report back.

Under 'Method', there would be an indication of a particular test utility or technique to be used.

The space given to external and internal test cases on the form is symbolic. Under normal circumstances, a separate sheet may be required.

The section on 'External Test Cases' should be filled in by the Team Member who is specifying the component. The attitude here is 'I don't care how your black box works: here are some situations I expect it to handle'.

The Team Member actually doing the development of this component creates the 'Internal Test Cases'. These reflect the way the component has been constructed and are to test out the branching and looping within the component.

'Record Key' may be either the genuine key of the appropriate piece of test data or any reference to the data to be used. Whether the specifier provides the actual data depends on what is said in paragraph two of the document.

UNIT TEST STRATEGY DOCUMENT

OBJECTIVES

1 To ensure that all functions identified in the program
specification are performed correctly.

2 To ensure that the structure of the program is correct.

RESPONSIBILITIES

Allocated to

External Test Data Design   —
External Test Data Preparation   —
External Test Data Predicted Results   —
Internal Test Data Design   —
Internal Test Data Preparation   —
Internal Test Data Predicted Results   —
Run Submission   —
Checking   —
Error Correction   —
Acceptance   —

LEVEL

1 Check all selection and iteration conditions.

2 Check all conditions for:
    precise condition value,
    just before condition value,
    just after condition value.

CONTROL POINTS

METHOD

EXTERNAL TEST CASES

  DESCRIPTION   **RECORD KEY**

INTERNAL TEST CASES

  DESCRIPTION   **RECORD KEY**

Fig. 7.5 Unit test document.

Chapter 3   System Test

When?   Normally started during design. It must be fully specified by compo-
                 nent development time. Parts of it must be available before model
                 construction.

What?   Figure 7.6 is an example of a document for this.

```
┌─────────────────────────────────────────────────────────────┐
│              SYSTEM TEST STRATEGY DOCUMENT                    │
├─────────────────────────────────────────────────────────────┤
│ OBJECTIVES                                                    │
│ 1  To ensure that the system is free from error before        │
│    release to the user.                                       │
│                                                               │
│ 2  To ensure that the user documentation is satisfactory      │
│    and reflects the actual system.                            │
│                                                               │
│ 3  To ensure that the system can be installed correctly       │
│    according to the documentation.                            │
├─────────────────────────────────────────────────────────────┤
│ RESPONSIBILITIES                        Allocated to          │
│                                                               │
│ External Test Data Design              —                      │
│ External Test Data Preparation         —                      │
│ External Test Data Predicted Results   —                      │
│ Internal Test Data Design              —                      │
│ Internal Test Data Preparation         —                      │
│ Internal Test Data Predicted Results   —                      │
│ Run Submission                         —                      │
│ Checking                               —                      │
│ Error Correction                       —                      │
│ Acceptance                             —                      │
├─────────────────────────────────────────────────────────────┤
│ LEVEL                                                         │
│ 1  Check that range and cross-reference validations are       │
│    working correctly.                                         │
│ 2  Check the correct production of all outputs.               │
│ 3  Check that any input or output interfaces work.            │
│ 4  Check each input type/combination and response.            │
├─────────────────────────────────────────────────────────────┤
│ CONTROL POINTS                                                │
│                                                               │
├─────────────────────────────────────────────────────────────┤
│ METHOD                                                        │
│                                                               │
├─────────────────────────────────────────────────────────────┤
│ EXTERNAL TEST CASES                                           │
│                                                               │
│   DESCRIPTION                       RECORD KEY                │
│                                                               │
├─────────────────────────────────────────────────────────────┤
│ INTERNAL TEST CASES                                           │
│                                                               │
│   DESCRIPTION                       RECORD KEY                │
│                                                               │
└─────────────────────────────────────────────────────────────┘
```

Fig. 7.6   System test document.

There may be many different types of test under the one heading of 'System Test'. Other types which may need to be done are:

Regression Test
Volume Test
Installability Test

A similar document would be needed for them.

INSTALLATION TEST STRATEGY DOCUMENT

OBJECTIVES

1 To ensure that installation instructions are adequate.

2 To ensure that the released product is complete.

3 To ensure that customization notes are correct.

RESPONSIBILITIES   Allocated to
External Test Data Design   —
External Test Data Preparation   —
External Test Data Predicted Results   —
Internal Test Data Design   —
Internal Test Data Preparation   —
Internal Test Data Predicted Results   —
Run Submission   —
Checking   —
Error Correction   —
Acceptance   —

LEVEL

1 Check that all installation prerequisites are
   defined in the documentation.
2 Check that the sequence of steps is correct and
   complete.
3 Check that the product links together after
   following the installation steps.

CONTROL POINTS

METHOD

EXTERNAL TEST CASES

DESCRIPTION   **RECORD KEY**

INTERNAL TEST CASES

DESCRIPTION   **RECORD KEY**

Fig. 7.7   Installation test document.

Chapter 4   Installation Test

When?   This is created during system test.

What?   Figure 7.7 shows the detail needed in this document.

Where the final system is to run on only the machine on which it is developed, you may decide that this is unnecessary.

Installation Test may be a collection of tests. Other tests at this point may be:

Conversion Test
Installation Build Test
Recovery Test
Performance Test

Chapter 5   Acceptance Test

When?

At the latest, this must be completed before any of the installation phase begins. The benefit of the philosophy behind this approach to documentation is that if we create the skeleton of all our documentation on day one of the project, any needs for, in this case, acceptance test can be written down at the time they occur, rather than be forgotten.

What?

Figure 7.8 gives an example of an acceptance test strategy document. Acceptance test may comprise several types of test such as:

User Acceptance Test
DP Operations Acceptance Test
External Procedure Test
Parallel Run
Pilot Test

Volume 5   User Manual

Chapter 1   System Description

When?

This should be done at the beginning of development, before component development.

What?

Overview of the system capabilities.
Explanation of general features of the system. These should include any use of standard codes and keys, and the meaning of any standard abbreviations to be used in the book.
Set-up routine. How to invoke the system, if it is a screen-based system, or how to submit work for a batch system.

Chapter 2   Schedule

When?

As for the other chapters.

ACCEPTANCE TEST STRATEGY DOCUMENT

OBJECTIVES

1 To ensure that the delivered product meets the agreed
   specification.

2 To prove to the user that the product is free from
   error.

3 To ensure that the user education has been carried
   out successfully.

RESPONSIBILITIES   Allocated to
External Test Data Design   –
External Test Data Preparation   –
External Test Data Predicted Results   –
Internal Test Data Design   –
Internal Test Data Preparation   –
Internal Test Data Predicted Results   –
Run Submission   –
Checking   –
Error Correction   –
Acceptance   –

LEVEL

1 Test against each acceptance criterion.

2 Test every input.

3 Produce and verify every output.

CONTROL POINTS

METHOD

EXTERNAL TEST CASES

DESCRIPTION   **RECORD KEY**

INTERNAL TEST CASES

DESCRIPTION   **RECORD KEY**

Fig. 7.8 Acceptance test document.

What?   Sequence of tasks. There may be divisions of this, such as:

Daily Processing Sequence
Monthly Processing Sequence
Year-end Processing Sequence
Special Event Processing Sequence

Figure 7.9 shows a matrix which can be used for each sequence.

SCHEDULE							
JOB IDENTITY	STEP	TIMING	INPUT AND SOURCE	OUTPUT AND DISTRIBUTION	RESPONSIBLE	CALL OUT	REFERENCE

Fig. 7.9 Schedule.

Chapter 3   Function Steps

When?   As for the other chapters.

What?   One section for each separate function.
Step-by-step description of the functions to be carried out by those involved in invoking and using the function. In a screen-based system, this should include pictures of all screen layouts presented to the user, an explanation of each prompt from the screen and the possible reply to be made. In a batch system, this should include pictures of all forms to be completed, explanation of all fields to be completed and how to submit the work.

Chapter 4   Error Messages and Recovery

When?   As for the other chapters.

What?   A list of all possible error messages from the system. This should be in alphanumeric order.
An explanation of the error.
Possible causes of the error.
Action to be taken.

Chapter 5   Glossary of Terms

When?   This can be started on day one of the project and updated at any time during the project with user or developer terminology which needs to be explained.

What?   An alphabetic list of all user or developer terms, which occur during
                         the project, and which should be explained for the benefit of future
                         users or the developers.

Volume 6   Installation Manual

Chapter 1   Prerequisites

When?   Commenced prior to the end of design.
                         Refined before the end of development.

What?   Work to be done in site preparation or preparation for installation of
                         the product.
                         Items whose presence will be required by installation time.
                         Expected quality level of ancillary products.
                         Version and modification numbers of supporting products.

Chapter 2   Bill of Material

When?   Prior to the end of system test.

What?   A listing of all the components which comprise the product or
                         system.

Chapter 3   Installation Steps

When?   Prior to the end of system test.

What?   Instructions on the installation or construction of the product or
                         system.

Chapter 4   Installation Test Steps

When?   Prior to the end of system test.

What?   A checklist of how to verify the correct construction of the product
                         prior to carrying out any conversions or acceptance tests.

Chapter 5   Customization Steps

When?   If applicable, prior to the end of development.

What?   Where the system can be modified to suit specific end-user needs or
                                different environments.
                                A list of the customization options.
                                A list of the items affected for each type of customization.
                                Instructions on how to carry out each type of customization.

INDEX